From Ashes to Healing

Betty Burke

New Wine Press

New Wine Ministries
PO Box 17
Chichester
West Sussex
United Kingdom
PO19 2AW

ISBN 978-1-905991-60-0

Typeset by **documen**, www.documen.co.uk
Cover design by CCD, www.ccdgroup.co.uk
Printed in the United Kingdom

CONTENTS

Foreword

I am writing my story for two reasons. Firstly, over many years now I have been given prophetic words that I am to write books. In May of 2010, as I was praying, I sensed the Lord was saying write the book NOW. The second reason that I want to tell this story is because HE has changed my life so much, given me hope, given me a reason to carry on, when the enemy's attacks were so great that the only option of escape at times seemed to be the gas oven, tablets, alcohol, or a very high wall could also seem a very good idea. He has given me forgiveness and a place to put all my guilt and shame so that it can all be washed away, gone forever, never to be remembered again. He has shown me so much of Himself and how much He loves us. I want to make HIM known. I am sharing my life, a lot of personal and private lessons I have learned over the 35 years of my walk with Jesus Christ, to testify to a wonderful Saviour, the Lord Jesus Christ of Nazareth, and also to help anybody going through similar things, to let you know that you can get free from your past and be a wonderful useful minister of the kingdom of God to this generation, that everybody and anybody equally can be used by the Lord, that you can hear His voice for yourself and that you can have a personal relationship with the creator of you, who loves you so much that He wants you to know Him, and He wants to know you, show you how much He loves you, to be assured that He has a plan for your life and it is a plan greater than ever you could dream about. No matter how broken you may be in your heart on the inside, Jesus Christ the Healer came to put you back together better than before, so that you can go from glory to glory experiencing His healing and freedom from hurts and emotional and physical pain and never be the same again. I want to thank my husband, Tom for his patience as I was writing this, and for all the support he has given me over the forty years of our marriage, all the challenges we worked through to get to forty years. He has come to the place of allowing me to be who I am, not an easy thing to do at all, and I honour and respect him greatly for that.

Betty Burke

Where am I?
by Andy Gray

The dog is barking, the children are looking for attention and trying to find their clean clothes for school, and the man of the house is just heading off to work.

After the shirt is found under a pile of Bible catalogues and the dog has found its ball in a box of cd's and the phone has stopped ringing for the fifth time, in walks a salesman with a bag and samples to add to the cause.

You would think that you were in the average English family home on a mad Monday morning, apart from the salesman.

However, rather than getting out a sales catalogue, he starts stirring the food on the cooker, no idea what it is, but it smells good.

Then to add to the muddle someone walks in from the street looking for help.

Have you worked it out yet?

No, I guess not.

Well, the answer is that it's a little shop in Walthamstow/ Leyton (district of London) just the size of a shop that sells sweets and cigarettes and not much space for much more. However, instead of the cigarettes and sweets, there are now books and Bibles, cards and pictures, bookmarks and gifts, videos and tapes, all sharing the message and the love of God. Spare space? You must be joking. There is stock piled up to the ceiling, under the table, on the table, and at some times holding up the table and not just in the shop. As you go through to the back, which is the home I talked about earlier, you find the same story with boxes tucked here, there and everywhere and catalogues on nearly every chair or table. Then you can somewhat picture the image of chaos that you feel.

However, what you find is a place of peace and love and joy that shares the love, joy and promise of a wonderful Saviour of whom the owner is wanting to share the message with the people of the area. A Bible is always open on the table and a video of some preacher sharing the message of God, usually to a large congregation.

The person calling in for help gets priority, the kids have gone to school and the shop is now open. However the need to see to someone's spiritual need gets priority so the rep just keeps stirring the pot, wondering if he will still be here at lunchtime or teatime to share in the meal which would often be shared by all who are around when it's time to eat.

The phone rings again with someone looking for something and the owner disappears upstairs to find what they are looking for (I never checked but I think even the beds are propped up with stocks of books and Bibles).

After hearing the phone ring several more times and an hour has passed and she has returned to the kitchen she then remembers that you are there. It's not that you are not important to the operation, it's just that things keep coming up that need her attention.

Eventually, after a number of hours and numerous interruptions, you leave the chaos for the tranquillity of your car and an order on the passenger seat but most of all and more important you take away with you the Spirit and love of God and the joy of seeing God's work alive and active in this part of London, praying that maybe, just maybe, there will one day be a chaotic oasis like this in every area of the world.

Andrew Gray
Sales Representative for Christian books and Bibles

Selling to Betty
by Malcolm Corden

During almost 20 years as a freelance representative for several Christian publishers and suppliers, I have had the almost unique experience of having the Good News Shop as a customer. In a previous life I was a member of Her Majesty's Royal Air Force and as such had experienced almost all the world could have thrown at me. I had gone to war, suffered for my faith at the hands of hardened servicemen and been separated from my family, often for many months at a time. Nothing could have prepared me, however, for The Good News Bible Bookshop and its owners Tom and Betty Burke.

Betty always met with reps in the kitchen, so one knew on entering the shop to go straight through the beaded curtain, which divided the shop and the flat, down the corridor and into the inner sanctum, the nerve centre, its table piled high with all manner of Christian literature. After my second or third visit I began to get familiar with the family and would regularly make tea and toast for myself and anyone who happened to be about, customers and staff alike. It was during a February visit, however, as I was just about to pop a couple of rounds of bread into the toaster, that Betty breezed past on the phone to Ireland (a regular source of frustration for reps). She pointed to a tin by the kettle and off she went. The tin contained Christmas cake which I didn't fancy much. I reverted to plan B. Betty appeared again, still on the phone. "Malcolm, that Christmas cake has to be eaten", she whispered, tucked the phone into her shoulder, took out the cake, cut me a large slice and was gone again. The name of the family dog escapes me but she was a lovely little thing and would always, thankfully on this occasion, readily appear when food was available. I surreptitiously fed the cake to the grateful dog bit by bit, leaving a few crumbs, as one does, as if I'd enjoyed it.

The Good News Bookshop remains a beacon of hope, a real ministry through which the Holy Spirit brings light, hope and healing to God's people and there are many stories that folk like me could tell about its work, but one sticks in my mind. I was just about to leave the store when a taxi pulled up outside. The driver came in and proceeded to engage Betty in private conversation. They hugged. Betty went straight to the till, took out some money, handed it to him and he was gone, one of the recent converts who had found his Saviour in the store I was later to find out. Faith in action.

Thank you, Betty, Tom, Jackie, Roy and all the other workers over the years who have poured out God's love through the ministry of the Word in E10.

Malcolm Corden
Sales Representative

A Prophetic Word by Lloyd Dwyer

"I see a barren landscape scarred and wasted after a cataclysmic natural event such as a massive hurricane or tsunami. In the middle of this I see a tree standing alone and flourishing in the midst of this desolation. That tree is your ministry and, like that solitary tree left standing, your ministry will continue to prosper and bear fruit in the desert of desolation."

Those were the words I received from the Holy Spirit during a seemingly ordinary discussion about the Christian book selling industry with Betty Burke several months ago. It took place during one of my periodic visits to the Good News bookshop in my capacity as an area sales manager. Betty asked me how I and my family were keeping (as she always does), and I replied that we were all okay and enjoying God's grace. Then the conversation switched to the Christian bookselling trade.

"How is the trade, Lloyd, and how is your company?" I was about to give her the stock answer in business jargon i.e. "Well Betty, as you know, the economic downturn continues to affect all sectors of retail adversely, and we are no exception, nonetheless we endeavour to service the market using 'best practice' principles, blah, blah, blah."All of a sudden I received a crystal clear vision of the Good News Bookshop in the scenario I described at the beginning of this piece. In an instant I switched from Dragon's Den mode to the prophetic and began to flow! To have done anything else would have been disobedient to the Holy Spirit's direction to speak from the heart of the Lord to my dear sister.

I have known Betty and Tom for fifteen years in my capacity as a sales representative for various companies, and never was a moment so defining and apt like the one I've just mentioned to describe the way I have seen this couple's ministry grow over the years. Testings and trials have come to them as it does to all of us who are kingdom children, however they have clearly adhered to the principles taught by the Apostle James:

JAMES 1:2-4

"My brethren, count it all joy when you fall into various trials, knowing that the testing of your faith produces patience. But let patience have its perfect work, that you may be perfect and complete lacking nothing."

Without a doubt they have lacked for nothing in terms of their ministry. The Lord has opened for them, and yes, closed doors to them, so that His perfect will would be made complete. The Holy Spirit has led people to work with them and continues to do so, all I may add of the highest calibre. They are Spirit filled and Spirit led workers exhibiting the fruit of the Spirit and representing not just the Good News bookshop but the Kingdom of God in a favourable light. You walk through the doors of the Good News bookshop and immediately you sense the Holy Spirit's presence.

The Ultimate Challenge

The key word that has been challenging me in recent years is the word *"Legacy"*. What will I leave behind in the years to come that will stand the test of time and give honour to God Almighty and His glorious Kingdom? Certainly not bricks and mortar, or titles and organisations with clever sounding names. No, my desire is to leave a Godly legacy in the hearts of those I have met and will meet before my time is up. Betty and Tom, I challenge you both to do the same. It is a challenge I strongly suspect you have both taken on with the same fervency that has driven you to continue the ministry of the Good News bookshop and the Healing Rooms.

May God's grace continue to give you peace, vision and purpose, and may you both hear those precious words from the Father when the work is done, *"Well done, good and faithful servant: you were faithful over a few things, I will make you ruler over many things: enter into the joy of your Lord"*.

Lloyd Dwyer
Sales Representative

1 *My Journey Begins*

In Dublin in 1948 on the 15th of January Elizabeth Hackett was born. There was no place for her as her mother was married to Jack Hackett who was not my father, further complicated by the fact that there was a sister of about 11 years old from this marriage. So I came in as a kind of intrusion into this marriage. My mother released me from her care when I was about 2 weeks old. My grandmother took me home to her house and adopted me. My father was her son, so she was my genuine grandmother.

My grandmother was then 70 years of age, a widow who raised her three children single-handed, two sons and a daughter. They had known little of their father who passed away from some illness in his early thirties. My father remained single, as did his brother, and their sister was divorced and had a son called Valentine.

My grandmother loved the Lord. She would teach me about Him and we would sing hymns at night together. I would sit by her knee and listen as she taught me about Samuel and the hymn written about him, "Hushed was the evening hymn" *(by James Drummond Burns – 19thCentury)*.

As I grew up though into the culture in which I was born, being illegitimate was a real stigma. It is hard to realize the effect of the stigma that was put on children like me, considering today more than half the children born are born outside marriage. To hide the embarrassment that was around me, I was kept out of the way, hidden, like a skeleton in the cupboard.... That meant a lot of hours playing alone, not having the benefit of playing with other children. I can even remember being christened. The religious background surrounding me was the "Church of Ireland", the Irish version of the Anglican Church. The tradition was that babies were christened, but because of the circumstances I was about 5 years of age, and even went to school rather later than the other children around. Eventually I was let out of the cupboard.

My grandmother had tried to help me grow in the Lord. and I was aware of spiritual things to a large extent, as attendance at church was regular. I used to play church afterwards; some kids played with dolls, I played standing in front of people preaching, reading and singing. Perhaps there are keys to our futures in our childhood play.

During these years I knew I was called to live in London, and I knew there were angels singing in the room, as the Lord made His call on my life clear. Despite the kindness experienced by a caring grandmother, she was unable to bring the household under peace and calm. Her children were all affected by alcoholism in one form or another, and drunkenness was a regular experience for a young girl. Shouting and noise brought a lot of insecurity and fear, with regular visits of the police to keep the peace.

As I grew older other influences came in and I began to turn my focus to boys, films, and unfortunately heavy drinking and smoking. I was thirteen when I bought my first cigarettes, Woodbines. I thought I was so grown up, but did not realize then the great struggle to give them up that would come when they became 30-40 a day. Also, I can remember drinking during my lunch-hour and a lot of evenings.

I found I was sick a lot, being unable to keep down the excess. I would usually end up vomiting up the evening's bevvy, and after escapades in the pub crawl, would find myself lying in bed with the room spinning around me. I would have to get up the following morning and clean up the mess from the night before. Still, this did not stop the need to dull the deep pain I felt on the inside so I carried on drinking, risking so much. Eventually joining an amateur dramatic society, I met my husband to be, Tom, who was nine years older than me. He began to give me stability, and the desire to save for a house, get married and have children began to replace the need for such heavy drinking. So my life became more stable from then on. I truly thank the Lord for sending this man to me, as I do not know where I would have ended up. My father died in sad circumstances due to the world of pubs, my aunt died from alcoholic poisoning and was dead for three days before being found, and my uncle too suffered from the effects of heavy drinking.

2 *Getting Married and Moving to England*

IIIIIIIIIIIIIIIIIIIIIIIIIIIIIIIIIIIIIIIIIIIIIIIIIIIIIIIIIIIIIIIIIIIIIIIIIIIIIIIIIIIIIIIIIIIIIIIIIIIIIIIIIIIIIIIIIIIIIIIIII

Tom and I got married in August 1970. Tom was raised a Roman Catholic so we were married in a Catholic church. Even then the Lord was arranging and speaking into our lives what 40 years later would fit into place more pieces of the jigsaw puzzles of our lives. When we were looking up our birth certificates we found a marriage certificate with the name of the priest who signed the certificate after marrying us. Father Raphael Clancy was his name, and apparently some people believe that the name of a healing angel is Raphel, (one of the names of the Lord is Jehovah Rapha, which means "the Lord who heals" – Exodus 15 v 25-26).

Tom was always very respectful of the fact that I was raised in a different spiritual environment, like the Church of Ireland, and he and I went to hear a well known evangelist of the day speaking in a peace vigil in St. Anne's Church of Ireland in Dawson Street, Dublin. Arthur Blessitt was known for carrying a huge cross all over the world. His testimony was that he was used of the Lord to bring many from the bars and nightclubs to finding a real life-changing relationship with Jesus Christ. I found him too much "in your face", with his strong American accent, leathers, fringes and cowboy boots which were all too much for my religious mind with

clergy safely dressed in long white and black robes. But
Tom was impressed and decided from that time on he would
attend the local church with me. I remember begging Tom,
please don't tell your mother as this could cause all sorts of
problems in the family, as they had hoped I would become
a Catholic, and now the opposite was happening. Our first
son, Jonathan, was born and he was christened into the local
Church of Ireland. This caused a lot of controversy and bad
feelings in the family, but we were both convinced this was
right for our new family.

Jonathan was the light of our lives, a delightful lively
little boy with sparkling eyes and a great smile and hearty
chuckle. I was unaware that my nice, secure, 3 bedroom
family life with savings for a rainy day was about to be
severely challenged as the Lord began to bring about His
call on my life.

It all began with a simple cold, a cold that would not go
away. Eventually it became pneumonia, and to take to bed
was the only option. Our beloved Jonathan had to be sent
to a relative to be looked after while I had treatment. In the
middle of this treatment I had what could be called a night
vision. It was so scary that I came back to myself completely
soaked in perspiration. In this vision of the night, I seemed
to leave my body and travel upwards and eventually came to
what I would call the outskirts of the throne of the Lord, the
creator of all things. I quickly realized that when we leave
this planet all former life and people fade quickly, and what
is in front is the only thing that matters. As I approached
eternity and what would seem to be heaven, I realized that
I could not enter this heavenly place where the Lord of
the universe resides, and I seemed to be moved away out
into this outer darkness, and as I spiralled backwards and
downwards into this darkness I realized that I was not going
to spend eternity with God the Father. Mercifully I began

to come back to myself with the utter shock I felt as the realization hit me that I could not enter this holy place. I was stunned for such a long time. I had been a fairly regular churchgoer and thought I was a reasonably good person who had not done anybody any real harm. I quickly realized that this was not sufficient and would not get me an entrance into this place we normally call heaven.

As I began to recover, we got our son Jonathan back again and we resumed our family life, but what I had experienced was a prime focus in my thinking and I began to ask all kinds of questions of clergy and people with whom I might find some answers but to no avail. The Lord had another plan, which was yet to unfold for Tom and me.

Tom was trained in electronics and worked for a company which was making workers redundant, and after a second employment and a further redundancy, we thought it might be a good idea to see if there were more jobs available across the water in London. We went across to have a look and Tom and I obtained a job running a newsagents. So the decision came to sell our house and move to the UK to set up home.

Tom went across by himself to train for about 7 weeks and I stayed in Dublin with Jonathan to pack up and put the house up for sale, little realizing we were about to step into the destiny and call for our lives.

During the time of Tom being away, as the house was sold quickly and the seven weeks were nearly over, the things of the spiritual realm began to start to become real and the Lord was speaking to me and Tom.

Our son Jonathan had always slept in exactly the same place at the window in his room. One night I had a strong sense that I needed to move his cot over to the other side of the room. This had never happened before as he always slept next to the window. But this night I felt the overwhelming need to move him away from the window. In the morning as I entered his room to pick him up for his breakfast I was stunned to see the floor covered with huge pieces of glass, and a large brick in the room that somebody had thrown at the window the night before. I was so shocked that I could hear the Lord and that He would speak about such down to earth matters like "move that cot"

As the Lord was beginning to make Himself known to me, I was learning that He wants to speak to us about all the concerns in our everyday life. I could not get this event out of my mind. The consequences if I had not moved Jonathan, he would surely have died. How would I have coped with this by myself? It left a huge impression on me, as I realized the Lord's intervention in our lives to save our son from possible death or certain injury, as I looked at the big chunks of glass that could have sliced through his little body. This made me search with even more determination to find a lasting relationship with the Lord. Upon settling in to life and work in London, we found a local Anglican church. My attention was riveted at what was being said, firstly because of the experience of not getting into heaven, and then by this experience of hearing spiritually not to put Jonathan's cot at the window that night in our house. Many surprises were on the way for me. One of the first was that the curate of this church, St. Mary's West Kensington, Michael Tungay, was preaching and making statements I had never heard anybody say before. "If you think that just sitting in this church every Sunday will get you into heaven you will be very disappointed." I remember feeling very angry. How dare he make such a statement like he knew what he was talking about.

3 *Born Again and Beginning to Understand At Last*

IIIIIIIIIIIIIIIIIIIIIIIIIIIIIIIIIIIIIIIIIIIIIIIIIIIIIIIIIIIIIIIIIIIIIIIIIIIIIIIIIIIIIIIIIIIIIIIIIIIIIIIIIIIIIIII

1975/6

As we were regularly attending St. Mary's Church, West Kensington, we noticed something different about this church. The people who attended were talking about the Lord as if He were very real to them, like they had a relationship with Him, and that He was answering their prayers regularly. I had many questions. A missionary called John Dean, who was staying at the church from India, came to our house for a meal. I could tell he carried a presence about him. It seemed to me as if you were entertaining the Lord Himself and when he left the presence of the Lord remained. I met a friend from the church called Ann. She helped me very much with answers to some more of my questions. Then I met a London City missioner who served at the church, John Rowland. One of my questions was how come the Lord is so real to these people, and yet so far away from me. And for the first time, it seemed to me, the light was beginning to be turned on as it was explained to me about this scripture.

*Jesus answered and said to him, "Most assuredly, I
say to you, unless one is born again, he cannot see the
Kingdom of God"*

John 3 v 3

This was the difference. You cannot have a relationship with
the Lord, until you ask the Lord Jesus Christ into your life,
accept His forgiveness for all offences against the Lord,
invite Him to be your personal Saviour and give your life
to Him. Now when this was explained to me, it made great
sense and I knew it was true, but I also knew it would mean
a big change in my life, and I did not think I was prepared
for that yet. So I kept putting it off, avoiding it, and this
decision made me very angry. The fear of surrendering to the
unknown found some reactions of mine to be very bizarre.

After about six weeks of struggling with the whole concept
of giving control of one's life over to somebody else, not
knowing what that could mean, something happened which
took me off the fence very quickly.

As we were living at the newsagents I had a particular
routine. Every evening I would put Jonathan in his cot in
his own room, having read him a story and seen him off to
sleep, then I would come into the kitchen, get the evening
meal ready to be cooked and I would lay the meat on the
grill or put it in the electric oven to be turned on after going
into the shop and locking up for the night. This particular
evening I remember putting Jonathan in bed in his cot as
usual, and when he was asleep I did the usual thing, putting
the meat and vegetables ready for cooking, to be turned
on when I came back, not realizing I had stored a thick
plastic shopping bag in the electric oven, and not taken it
out. I must unknowingly have turned it all on and when I
returned from locking up the shop the whole place was full
of thick, black smoke. We had to open all the windows to

let these black clouds out and we were coughing for ages afterwards. Thankfully Jonathan's door was a very tight fit and his door was closed, so no smoke actually got into his room at all.

I realized Jonathan could have been killed and we could have lost him for the second time in his short two years of life.

A new life 1976

It was then I realized that I must now give my life to the Lord and be born again, because I was making such a mess of everything by myself, so I knew I needed the Lord so badly and the time was now. The Bible says that today is the day of salvation. That means don't put it off.

As soon as I could get everything calmed down and the meal eaten, I got down on my knees by my side of the bed and I confessed all the sins I could remember to the Lord, and I invited Him into my heart, into my spirit, to rule there, in the simplest words really. Although there were no fireworks or blue flashes, I knew that I had done the right thing and there was a tremendous peace on the inside. The next day I went shopping and I had a shopping trolley on wheels with me, and as I walked up the hill towards home suddenly I had my first revelation. I just knew all my sins had fallen away and I was free. I knew that all my sins were completely forgiven: it was like a great burden had fallen off my shoulders. I knew that if I were to leave this planet any time I would be able to enter that place we call heaven where the throne of God is. The entrance was paid by Jesus Christ on that cross 2,000 years ago.

I would have to say that everything seemed different, I saw the world from a different place. The bible came alive for me and I began my walk that I am still walking 35 years later.

I had another revelation a few weeks later, as I was looking out the window facing the tube station. When the next tube train came in, hundreds of people came off the train and walked and ran down the steps. The Lord began to bring to life the following scripture.

> *12 I looked when He opened the sixth seal, and behold,[e]*
> *there was a great earthquake; and the sun became black*
> *as sackcloth of hair, and the moon[f] became like blood.*
> *13 And the stars of heaven fell to the earth, as a fig tree*
> *drops its late figs when it is shaken by a mighty wind. 14*
> *Then the sky receded as a scroll when it is rolled up, and*
> *every mountain and island was moved out of its place. 15*
> *And the kings of the earth, the great men, the rich men,*
> *the commanders,[g] the mighty men, every slave and every*
> *free man, hid themselves in the caves and in the rocks of*
> *the mountains, 16 and said to the mountains and rocks,*
> *"Fall on us and hide us from the face of Him who sits*
> *on the throne and from the wrath of the Lamb! 17 For*
> *the great day of His wrath has come, and who is able*
> *to stand?"*

Revelation 6 v 12-17

It seemed that one day crowds of people, just like the ones coming from the train now, would have to face the music of meeting the Lamb unprepared, and they too were just as shocked as I was of the reality of eternal things and they too wanted to hide from the One who loves them so much.

Our own shop and business 1976

As we were working long hours for somebody else, Tom and I wondered if we should work for ourselves and get our own little shop and be self-employed, so we started looking in the newspapers for a business for sale. We looked at several and for some reason which I cannot remember now, we seemed to like a little confectionary, tobacconist shop in the High Road in Leyton. We leased these premises and moved in and it seemed to be a very good investment. As we had sold our house in Dublin we put all the proceeds from this sale into this business. So all we owned in the world now were these premises in Leyton.

4

An Encounter With The Holy Spirit

IIIIIIIIIIIIIIIIIIIIIIIIIIIIIIIIIIIIIIIIIIIIIIIIIIIIIIIIIIIIIIIIIIIIIIIIIIIIIIIIIIIIIIIIIIIIIIIIIIIIIIIIIIIIIIIIIIIIIIIIIIIII

I carried on worshipping every week and began to grow in the Lord. I was now pregnant with my second son, Peter. My friend Ann was going through a rough time and I thought I would go and pray for her at "the London Healing Mission" (now called the Christian Healing Mission). When I was there I went and knelt down at the communion rail for the minister (Roy Jeremiah) to pray for me (actually for Ann) and I started to explain my reason for being there. He asked me if I would like to receive the baptism with the Holy Spirit. I had no idea what that meant but how could one say No to more of God? It is so interesting how the Lord chooses significant places in which to touch us, that will have a meaning for us in the future, for instance, this place where people were prayed for, seeking healing both physical and spiritual, as ministering healing ourselves would come to be a part of our lives in the future. This kind man prayed for me to receive the precious gift of the person of the Holy Spirit. I did not understand anything about the Holy Spirit or His gifts, so on the train home to Leyton I thought I had better get to know what all this meant and I began to read about when the Holy Spirit first came to the Church.

LUKE 24 v 49

*Jesus speaking, "Behold, I send the Promise of My
Father upon you; but tarry in the city of Jerusalem[i] until
you are endued with power from on high."*

ACTS 1 v 4-5

*4 And being assembled together with them, He (Jesus)
commanded them not to depart from Jerusalem, but to
wait for the Promise of the Father, "which," He said,
"you have heard from Me;5 for John truly baptized with
water, but you shall be baptized with the Holy Spirit not
many days from now."*

ACTS 2 v 1 – 21

The Coming of the Holy Spirit

*1 When the Day of Pentecost had fully come, they were
all with one accord in one place. 2 And suddenly there
came a sound from heaven, as of a rushing mighty wind,
and it filled the whole house where they were sitting.
3 Then there appeared to them divided tongues, as of
fire, and one sat upon each of them. 4 And they were all
filled with the Holy Spirit and began to speak with other
tongues, as the Spirit gave them utterance.*

The Crowd's Response

*5 And there were dwelling in Jerusalem Jews, devout
men, from every nation under heaven. 6 And when this
sound occurred, the multitude came together, and were
confused, because everyone heard them speak in his own
language. 7 Then they were all amazed and marvelled,
saying to one another, "Look, are not all these who speak
Galileans? 8 And how is it that we hear, each in our own
language in which we were born? 9 Parthians and Medes
and Elamites, those dwelling in Mesopotamia, Judea and*

*Cappadocia, Pontus and Asia, ¹⁰ Phrygia and Pamphylia,
Egypt and the parts of Libya adjoining Cyrene, visitors
from Rome, both Jews and proselytes, ¹¹ Cretans and
Arabs—we hear them speaking in our own tongues the
wonderful works of God." ¹² So they were all amazed
and perplexed, saying to one another, "Whatever could
this mean?"*
    ¹³ Others mocking said, "They are full of new wine."

Peter's Sermon
*¹⁴ But Peter, standing up with the eleven, raised his voice
and said to them, "Men of Judea and all who dwell in
Jerusalem, let this be known to you, and heed my words.
¹⁵ For these are not drunk, as you suppose, since it is
only the third hour of the day. ¹⁶ But this is what was
spoken by the prophet Joel:*

*¹⁷ ' And it shall come to pass in the last days,
    says God,
That I will pour out of My Spirit on all flesh;
Your sons and your daughters shall prophesy,
Your young men shall see visions,
Your old men shall dream dreams.
¹⁸ And on My menservants and on My maidservants
I will pour out My Spirit in those days;
And they shall prophesy.
¹⁹ I will show wonders in heaven above
And signs in the earth beneath:
Blood and fire and vapour of smoke.
²⁰ The sun shall be turned into darkness,
And the moon into blood,
Before the coming of the great and awesome day of
    the Lord.
²¹ And it shall come to pass*

That whoever calls on the name of the Lord
Shall be saved.'

I sought the Lord earnestly for several weeks after that for more of Him, and for a spiritual language which I believed I could receive because I knew the disciples did.

I knew something had happened to me though, because for the first time my fear of sharing the gospel had left me. And in the window of the confectionary tobacconist I put the first Christian book for sale. It got sold very soon and then we began to replace it. I was no longer ashamed to proclaim the One who had saved me and changed my life. And as the scripture said in Acts 1 v 5 *"not many days hence",* about six weeks after the prayer, I was in bed and one of the children started to cry. Tom said, "I'll go," and as he closed the door the whole room filled up with the presence and glory and joy of the Lord. Next thing I knew these words came to me, into my mind, and as I began to speak them out more and more came and they have been coming ever since. I realized I was now speaking in a language I had never learned, one given to me by the Holy Spirit. Just like in the book of Acts, Chapter 2. The Apostles were waiting in that upper room for Him to come just like Jesus promised He would. The Holy Spirit came with wind, fire, a new sound, languages and boldness. Verse 7 in the Amplified Bible says about the people of the city, *"They were beside themselves with amazement"* and the city of Jerusalem was turned upside down, never to be the same again.

I found this a very important gift to have, as there are times when we don't know how to pray, and the Holy Spirit can pray through us. There were other differences in my life, because experience alone isn't enough. There has to be fruit as well. Jesus makes it so clear in the New Testament that He is requiring fruit from that experience as well.

I Never Knew You

MATTHEW 7 v 21-23

> [21] *"Not everyone who says to Me, 'Lord, Lord,' shall enter the kingdom of heaven, but he who does the will of My Father in heaven.[22] Many will say to Me in that day, 'Lord, Lord, have we not prophesied in Your name, cast out demons in Your name, and done many wonders in Your name?'[23] And then I will declare to them, 'I never knew you; depart from Me, you who practice lawlessness!'*

The Holy Spirit is not just a language or even gifts. He is a person. For instance, when the wind blows we cannot see the wind, but we see the effect of it in the tree by the leaves and branches moving about. We never think that the tree is moving its branches by itself, we know it is the effect of the wind upon it. And when the wind is strong enough, we can see the evidence by the tree ending up on the ground. Some people shake, fall on the floor, prophesy, see pictures, visions, get impressions, or feel the heat of healing flowing through them. The Holy Spirit is not just these manifestations. This could be the evidence that He is on or in that person. That is the effect He brings upon them. But, of course, the fruit in our life is what He is also looking for too, so we need gifts and fruit working together. The main difference for me was that I found that before this time with the Holy Spirit I found it very hard to talk about my faith. I was very shy and a bit embarrassed about my faith, and it was hard for me to share the truth of the gospel of salvation, to be able to explain the new birth, and bring people to Jesus. But after this experience with the Holy Spirit, I found a new freedom and boldness, that what people thought about me was not my first priority, but that they could hear about this wonderful

Jesus and the eternal life they could have in heaven with Him, not just in the future but now. I wasn't so bothered or fearful about what people would think of me anymore.

MATTHEW 3 v 8

Therefore bear fruits worthy of repentance

MATTHEW 7 v 16 – 20

[16] You will know them by their fruits. Do men gather grapes from thornbushes or figs from thistles? [17] Even so, every good tree bears good fruit, but a bad tree bears bad fruit. [18] A good tree cannot bear bad fruit, nor can a bad tree bear good fruit. [19] Every tree that does not bear good fruit is cut down and thrown into the fire. [20] Therefore by their fruits you will know them.

5

Giving up the "Ciggies", 1981

More and more we began to put Christian books and Bibles in the bookshop with the help of Mr. Farrell from the Bethnal Green Medical Mission Bookshop, now called *Books for Life*. This wonderful man trusted us with some of his stock on a sale or return basis. I remember so well selling our first Bible. It was one of the ones the Trinitarian Bible Society print and it cost 50p then. I remember vividly jumping up and down with excitement for ages after that. Finally came the challenge to stop selling tobacco once and for all. Tom and I became more and more uncomfortable with selling this product because of the harm it could do to people, and as Christians we were not comfortable with making a living in this fashion. The final crux came one day, when on the same day three different people said they were so glad to see us selling cigarettes because they knew it must be OK for them to smoke as we were Christians, who the Lord was using, and we made our living from cigarettes. One man even said that he could support us by smoking and buying his ciggies here. We knew immediately that even though all we owned was in this business, and now had three small children to support, we could not carry on in this way. So after praying with several Christians, we felt we were being led by the Lord, and decided that from the next day we would buy no more cigarette stock, but sell all we had and end it there, then what? A tobacconist without tobacco would not be much good.

After about three months of only selling sweets and ice cream, and the odd book and Bible, we finally came to a halt financially. All our savings were gone, and we were in a pretty desperate place. People could see our difficulties and many times we would find money on the floor, from people putting it in the letterbox overnight, and open the mail and find gifts of money, which was so encouraging as the Lord was encouraging us to keep going. A gentleman who had a shoe shop in Ilford asked us lots of questions about our step of faith, and, bless him, he shared our predicament in his local church the next Sunday morning at the Elim church, and at the end of the meeting a man asked for our name and address. It transpired that there was a wonderful man named Keith Scott who had a bookshop about 15 minutes drive away from us, had being praying for somebody to replace the work he had going with his Christian bookshop, but as his lease was expiring soon he had to move away. We were put in touch with each other, and Keith asked us to pray about it and see if we felt the Lord would want us to turn this shop fully into a Christian bookshop. Well, after praying for about a week, we felt this would be great. I loved Christian books so much, I would often have a book in one hand and be ringing up fags and matches with the other. So I was very excited about the prospect, as was Tom too. But we had no money to buy stock to fill it with Christian books, because the shop was fairly empty by now. Keith said, "If you feel it is right I will let you have a portion of my stock and you will not have to pay for them until you sell them, and then you can give me the cost and you keep the profit". It is hard to put into words the excitement and gratefulness we felt as thousands of books arrived at the shop and landed in the middle of the floor. Tom got to work and made shelves

with wood, hammer and nails. And so we started our walk
in obedience.

His Place

At around the same time we were praying about the shop and
our future with it, some friends made a way for us to have
a little holiday break near Skegness, and there we found a
wonderful Christian Bookshop called His Place, with a Café
attached, and a place for ministry upstairs, and I knew when
I saw that premises, that the Lord was sowing a seed in my
heart for what is possible, even that we could have something
similar in Leyton. As Tom and I were spending time praying
about it all, Tom heard the Lord say, "I have called you into
this place"

Money in the door

When we had taken this step of faith to be obedient, I would
love to tell you that we had no more problems after that, but
it was like the beginning of problems. When things would get
really tight financially we could come down in the morning
and find money on the floor where people would drop gifts
in through the letterbox, or we would open a letter and find a
cheque inside. It was exciting to see answers to our prayers.
We tried never to make our needs known to anybody and we
never asked for money. Only the Father knew the real truth
of our situation.

Tom going to work, 1986-1993

Tom got to the place where there was no alternative but to
go to work. He got a job working in the booking office for
London Underground. He worked there for seven years and

this saved the bookshop and helped our budget so much. The bookshop began to take off when Tom started to work. All we are doing today is because he was willing to make this sacrifice. It was not easy for him as the shop had been his work and his home and he had put a lot into trying to build it up, so he handed it over to me. I was now totally running the bookshop and trying to raise the boys at the same time. Tom looked after the finances and paid the bills. I dreaded the telephone ringing, and the embarrassment of having to explain we did not have any money to pay what we owed the company at the moment. Most were polite after promises of as soon as Tom gets paid we will send the money. One supplier told us that if we did not pay up immediately they would see us in court. The man most dreaded coming down the street was the postman with his brown envelopes and the red stamp inside saying "overdue". We received so many red notices we could have wallpapered the kitchen with them. There were varying amounts of days with threats. 7 days or else, 10 days or else, 14 days or else, 28 days or else.

The worst day ever was the day the electricity man came in to turn off the electricity. I was so embarrassed, red in the face, and begged him not to turn it off, telling him we had three small children, and he obliged and left the shop with promises to pay as soon as we could ringing in his ears. That was one of my deepest valleys and the other was when somebody brought in some pots of food and said "hope this is OK for you, it might have gone off". I took it and we prayed over it and I'm glad to say we are all alive and kicking today.

After about six months we began so see a change take place. I learned many valuable lessons from that time of financial struggle. One thing is, if I don't have the money then I won't buy. I got rid of everything we did not need to spend money on. Even the television went for about six months, so we would not have to pay the rent on the television set and the licence fee. I learnt to get out of debt and never entered it again. The Lord is so faithful to us and He can turn even the worst things around for His glory.

Jumble sales

Saturday was jumble sale day and I can still remember the smell to this day of piles of clothes on top of tables. I remember a lovely looking jacket and I pulled a sleeve from the pile only to find another lady had the other sleeve and she was pulling very hard. I was tempted to pull even harder but then I remembered Jesus and I let go. Humorous now. Tom was not always "best pleased" with me returning with the large black bag saying "MORE CLOTHES". I remember one of our sons being told, "I had a jumper like that, but my mother put it in the jumble sale".

Lydia, 1981

As we were making the decision to change from a tobacconist to a Christian bookshop, I was about to learn a very important lesson in the way the Lord speaks to us, and how we need to discern how He is speaking to us and the context into which He is speaking. I was in bed one night around 10.00pm with Tom beside me. I was three months pregnant. I heard the Lord say to me very clearly, "Lydia". That was all He said, just the name. The first mistake I made was not asking Him what He meant. Instead I banged my husband in the ribs and said to him, the Lord has said to me the name "Lydia" .... that means we are going to have a little girl and call her "Lydia". The second mistake I made was I told everyone without checking with the Lord first. "We are going to have a little girl and we are going to call her Lydia." I told all the customers in the shop, the church, my friends, everybody I knew. Then the time came for deliverance of my baby. After the moment of birth the nurse said, "you have a lovely baby boy", whom the Lord then told us to call "James Andrew". He was so beautiful and a very good weight. He still has big muscles today. Now my dilemma was that I was so sure I had heard the Lord, as it was so clear. In my utter embarrassment I put all prophetic hearing from the Lord away in a locked drawer, promising myself no more "hearing from God". I was totally mystified and felt thrown into a kind of vicious circle of no answers. Our brilliant James grew up into a lovely boy. I had always planned for boys anyway, and I was not disappointed in him in any way.

"But God". Many times in Scripture we see this expression. "But God". The story is not finished because often when we are finished with something, and think it is all over and finished, the Lord has much to say, and twelve years later, I was with Jonathan, James's oldest brother, in Birmingham visiting him, and went with him to church on the Sunday. The pastor called me to the front. Now Mike Price, the pastor, knew I was Jonathan's mum, and that we had a bookshop, but that was all. He began to prophesy over me and in the middle of this prophecy which lasted for four minutes (you can get a lot of words into four minutes) he began to say, the Lord speaking through him, "you have heard me speaking to you concerning the ministry of Lydia. She was a business woman who sold the things of the king, she was a woman of influence, etc. etc." I was so amazed at the precision of the Lord, and so relieved that I had in fact heard Him. But I had put what He said into the context of my physical condition, instead of my spiritual condition. The Lord was not calling my child "Lydia" but He was calling me "Lydia". So a good lesson learnt and a renewed confidence in hearing the voice of the Lord. I have to say also that I am so thankful for a man who can hear the Lord with such clarity. It helped me beyond measure and put all my confusion to rest on this issue. Isn't the Lord good?

Now getting back to London and the task in hand of building a business and a ministry, I would love to be able to testify that it was always easy, but quite the opposite was the case. In fact obedience is not always easy, even when you have the word of the Lord to stand on. We asked the Lord for a word of confirmation meaning we wanted to be sure we were doing the right thing and not just our own idea. And he gave us the name "Good News Shop " and this scripture:

MICAH 4 v 1- 2
¹ Now it shall come to pass in the latter days
That the mountain of the Lord's house
Shall be established on the top of the mountains,
And shall be exalted above the hills;
And peoples shall flow to it.
² Many nations shall come and say,
* Come, and let us go up to the mountain of the Lord,*
To the house of the God of Jacob;
He will teach us His ways,
And we shall walk in His paths."
For out of Zion the law shall go forth,
And the word of the Lord from Jerusalem.

After 30 years of trading and ministering to people we can now say that many nations have flowed in and we have sent many materials all over the world and many people have come to know the Lord.

The first seven years were the most difficult, but we learnt to begin to trust even when it seemed so impossible. Customers would give generous gifts to us. Some would buy books and also give the children money, and often be very generous to Tom and me in so many ways. We often felt so blessed and cared about by the Christian community. One time a collection of tins came in with no labels on. As I was putting meals together, the boys would ask "What's for dinner Mum?" I would reply, "Not sure yet ...."

When we would have large bills waiting to be paid, customers would come in from time to time and buy very large amounts of books so they would be paid.

Paul said he learnt to be abased and to abound.

PHILIPPIANS 4 v 12 – 13
> *[12] I know how to be abased, and I know how to abound.*
> *Everywhere and in all things I have learned both*
> *to be full and to be hungry, both to abound and to*
> *suffer need.[13] I can do all things through Christ[b] who*
> *strengthens me.*

I would say we certainly learnt both.

After seven years of struggle and grappling with finances, Tom felt he should go out to work and leave me to run the bookshop, and as his earnings began to pay for our food and living expenses the shop began to take off, and we began to get straightened out financially, a gift Tom gave us that I will always be so grateful for. His part and sacrifice saved the ministry we now have running to this day.

Some of the incidents are funny now as I look back at and wonder how on earth we raised three boys in such circumstances of running a home with husband Tom and sons Jonathan, Peter and James.

The man with a gun

The following incident showed me how powerful the gift of tongues can be and I began to realize that this scripture sums up how much the Lord steps in when we cry out using the gifts that He has provided for us to walk in.

ROMANS 8 v 26 – 27

26 Likewise the Spirit also helps in our weaknesses. For we do not know what we should pray for as we ought, but the Spirit Himself makes intercession for us[b] with groanings which cannot be uttered.

27 Now He who searches the hearts knows what the mind of the Spirit is, because He makes intercession for the saints according to the will of God.

Tom, our three boys and myself were in the shop one day and a man came in with a gun. He locked himself in by closing the bolt over the wooden shop-front we had then. Nobody could now get in or out of the shop. The man came behind the counter towards our living accommodation and he hit Tom over the head with the gun. Tom fell to the ground and he started to bleed from his head. He came to the bottom of the stairs and I saw his gun. He told me to go back, and I began to pace back and forth across the floor upstairs and to shout at the top of my voice in the tongues of the Holy Spirit as He gave me utterance, and the next thing we knew the man took off running out of the shop quickly. He ran away without trying to steal anything. I believe the angels were activated by the Lord and he must have seen something or felt something that terrified him. The Bible tells us in that well known scripture:

ROMANS 8 v 28

And we know that all things work together for good

to those who love God, to those who are the called
according to His purpose.

The end result of this, after Scotland Yard had come around taken pictures and fingerprints, was that the local newspaper came round and wrote a story on the bookshop with a picture and put it on the back page. The article was called, "BAD NEWS FOR GUNMAN AT THE GOOD NEWS SHOP". So now the whole borough of Waltham Forest knew there was a Christian Bookshop in the area. Yet another way the Holy Spirit helped me by using this gift of His by speaking in tongues was when Tom would have to work shifts, sometimes late at night, or through the night. We were going through a time of having horrible phone calls with unclean noises and phrases that were very disgusting and I found that if I were to pray very loudly in tongues in the name of Jesus down the telephone, without fail it always worked. You could sense they were surprised and taken aback, even afraid. They always put the telephone down quickly, never ringing back. So the Holy Spirit always helps us in our infirmities (difficulties), even when we are alone and scared and don't know what to do.

6 *A World of Dreams, 1990*

The Bible is full of the different ways the Lord communicates with His people, and one of the ways He communicates with me is through dreams. I heard somebody teach that if the Lord speaks to you in dreams it is because He can't get your attention during the day, like you won't spend any time with Him, therefore the only time He can get your attention is when you are asleep. I must say that I don't personally find that to be true. For me it seems that He is a God of such variety and creativity that He likes to give us different experiences and lessons in hearing Him and us having the fun of working out exactly what He is meaning and learning new things about Him.

The experience I shared earlier about coming up some kind of tunnel towards heaven, I don't believe was a dream, I believe it was a real experience like a trance or a night vision. Peter, in the book of Acts, while he was praying saw and experienced the sheet of animals coming down from heaven.

ACTS 10 v 9-16 – PETER'S VISION

⁹ The next day, as they went on their journey and drew near the city, Peter went up on the housetop to pray, about the sixth hour.¹⁰ Then he became very hungry and wanted to eat; but while they made ready, he fell into a

trance [11] and saw heaven opened and an object like a
great sheet bound at the four corners, descending to him
and let down to the earth. [12] In it were all kinds of four-
footed animals of the earth, wild beasts, creeping things,
and birds of the air. [13] And a voice came to him, "Rise,
Peter; kill and eat."

    [14] But Peter said, "Not so, Lord! For I have never
eaten anything common or unclean."

    [15] And a voice spoke to him again the second time,
"What God has cleansed you must not call common."[16]
This was done three times. And the object was taken up
into heaven again.

In my dream I could see that I was walking towards the
bookshop down the High Road, and as I approached it I
remembered experiencing a feeling of such urgency over me
to purchase this shop (we were leasing it at the time) and it
was almost as though if we lingered over the decision to buy
we could miss the opportunity. It was so important that we
did make it a priority, and I knew I could feel emotionally
the seriousness of the situation. I had the distinct impression
that it was very important to buy this building. I had been a
person who was raised in a church that believed the second
coming of the Lord was imminent and that not getting into
debt was really important. And so Tom and I would have
been very hesitant about taking on a brand new mortgage,
and as we did not have any deposit, savings, or financial
backup and taking our ages into account it was a very scary
prospect indeed. In the morning I shared it with Tom and we
prayed for some more guidance. When we moved into the
shop we had leased the premises and bought the business.
As we were praying about it, two days later a letter arrived
from the landlord's daughter saying her father had died and
they were giving us a chance to buy before they put it on the

market. On the following Sunday evening we went to visit a church about 10 miles away. We had never been to this church before and as far as we knew nobody knew us there either. During the meeting the pastor's wife, who we now know to be Rita, said that while praying on the Saturday night she felt impressed to read a passage from the Bible on the Sunday at one of the services. But in the morning she knew by the Holy Spirit's impression that this passage of scripture was for the evening service, that there would be somebody there that the Lord wanted to speak to through this particular passage. This is the passage she read.

JEREMIAH 32 v 6-15 – JEREMIAH BUYS A FIELD

> *6 And Jeremiah said, "The word of the Lord came to me, saying, 7 'Behold, Hanamel the son of Shallum your uncle will come to you, saying, "Buy my field which is in Anathoth, for the right of redemption is yours to buy it."' 8 Then Hanamel my uncle's son came to me in the court of the prison according to the word of the Lord, and said to me, 'Please buy my field that is in Anathoth, which is in the country of Benjamin; for the right of inheritance is yours, and the redemption yours; buy it for yourself.' Then I knew that this was the word of the Lord. 9 So I bought the field from Hanamel, the son of my uncle who was in Anathoth, and weighed out to him the money—seventeen shekels of silver. 10 And I signed the deed and sealed it, took witnesses, and weighed the money on the scales. 11 So I took the purchase deed, both that which was sealed according to the law and custom, and that which was open; 12 and I gave the purchase deed to Baruch the son of Neriah, son of Mahseiah, in the presence of Hanamel my uncle's son, and in the presence of the witnesses who signed the purchase deed, before all the Jews who sat in the court of the prison.*

[13] "Then I charged Baruch before them, saying, [14] 'Thus says the Lord of hosts, the God of Israel: "Take these deeds, both this purchase deed which is sealed and this deed which is open, and put them in an earthen vessel, that they may last many days." [15] For thus says the Lord of hosts, the God of Israel: "Houses and fields and vineyards shall be possessed again in this land."'

The pastor's wife was called Rita. This wonderful lady who obeyed the voice of the Lord and ministered to us so deeply, said she knew that the Lord was saying to somebody at that meeting that they were to buy property. I wept so much at the way He speaks to us so definitely and clearly if we will just pay attention.

PROVERBS 4 v 20 – 22

[20] My son, give attention to my words; Incline your ear to my sayings. [21] Do not let them depart from your eyes;Keep them in the midst of your heart; [22] For they are life to those who find them, And health to all their flesh.

Kensington Temple, 1992-1999

We were worshipping in Kensington Temple, Notting Hill Gate, a Pentecostal Church that encouraged all its members to be trained up and functioning in the gifts of the Holy Spirit. Colin Dye, the senior minister, was teaching about the fact that some of us can just be sitting in the church week after week but never learning how to minister to others, and to be an effective Christian who knows what their gifts and callings are. Leadership is about serving the Church, as well as the Church serving the leaders. This was so totally new to me, as I had always served the pastor and never saw it the other way around. He was not saying that we should not serve our leaders, but they were also there to serve us and help us to find the call, gifts and destiny the Lord has put on our life and to walk in it.

We travelled a long way across the city for seven years many times a week and it was such a learning time for us, a wonderful season of learning how to hear the voice of the Lord and to obey and to go deeper into the things of the Lord. Tom and I were going through being trained for the ministry team of this church and the training we received has been invaluable. I will always be grateful to Colin Dye and all the other leaders and ministers for all they put into us. This has been for us fruit that has remained.

JOHN 15 v 16

You did not choose Me, but I chose you and appointed you that you should go and bear fruit, and that your fruit should remain.

We were not yet released from our training to actually be hands on workers at the end of meetings. It was in this time in my life that I remember this dream and how the Lord wanted to instruct me further to get ready for this new season. There was a large team of pastors and leaders in this church, and in the dream a particular pastor (who was on the staff at the time) called me forward and had us face the congregation (which was anything from 800 to 1,000 on a Sunday morning) to minister at the front of the church after the message was preached. I knew I was not ready. I felt so intimidated and unsure of myself, there were many things in my heart that needed to be cleaned out, so I knew I had to spend some time with the Lord in repentance and preparation for this time ahead, realizing that I needed to pay attention in my walk with the Lord to be ready. It's not so good when someone needs prayer now, immediately, and then we

can't pray because we are not ready. We should always be
ready for any need a person may have. A few weeks later it
happened exactly as in the dream. Sunday morning came and
for the first time this particular pastor called all the ministry
team down to the front to face the congregation and called
them forward if they needed prayer for anything. You really
felt you were on display to everybody. I was so glad of the
warning in the dream to be prepared for any situation. It was
such a lesson to me, the faithfulness of a God who cares for
His people He wants to prepare us for what is ahead.

Child's ears healed

Soon healing became a subject of study in the scriptures, as
in this church we saw quite a lot of healing taking place.
My interest in healing grew and I read many books on the
subject. As Tom and I carried on in the ministry team, there
were times when the presence of the Lord was so strong it
was hard to stay on your feet. One of many prayer times
stands out particularly. For instance, on one of the evenings
there was a very strong anointing and the presence of the
Lord was tangibly there. I was so awed at His nearness.
It seemed to me that you could just reach out and touch
Him. As I was praying, like we did at the time when the
congregation stood in line to be prayed for, and as I walked
down the line, there was a child about ten years of age and
as I laid my hand on her head, I had no idea of any physical
problem she may have had. She fell to the floor laughing and
was very overcome by the Holy Spirit. She eventually got
up from the floor and her parents found me and told me that
when she got up from the floor, they removed both hearing
aids that she had in her ears, as she apparently was born with
about 10% hearing and always wore these hearing aids. Her
parents told me she could hear perfectly now, and I am told

she still hears to this day. It was so interesting that I did not notice her hearing aids and I did not pray for healing. The Lord Himself ministered healing to her in His own way. I have always been so grateful for this seven-year season in my life. It was a season of awakening and learning which meant such a huge transformation, and for Colin Dye's teaching, risk taking and gifting there is always a place of thankfulness in my heart.

7 *The Bookshop Begins to Take Off*

IIIIIIIIIIIIIIIIIIIIIIIIIIIIIIIIIIIIIIIIIIIIIIIIIIIIIIIIIIIIIIIIIIIIIIIIIIIIIIIIIIIIIIIIIIIIIIIIIIIIIIIIIIIIIIIIIIIIIIII

We continued to increase and increase in the bookshop and eventually we were able to afford to employ an assistant, and eventually enough staff to run the shop completely. Also there were some people who came to help us on a voluntary basis. People like Teri and others heard the Lord asking them to serve with us for a season. We always managed from then on to keep on top of our bills. We have a great reputation to this day for keeping all our finances up to date and will always continue to pray for that testimony. We bought a video library and it grew very quickly, and eventually we had one of the biggest in the country and people came from near and far to receive teaching from these videos. Only when we get to Glory will we know the full impact of this ministry that was the Lord's idea. When the God Channel became available, among other factors, the need no longer was there, so we closed it down. We sent books all over the world. Bags with our "Jesus is Alive" written in purple on a white bag became seen all over the city of London and other cities too, even as far as Moscow. Once, in Ghana, a person from Walthamstow was walking down a country road, and found the other person on the country road knew the bookshop. The Lord amazed us beyond our wildest dreams with this, using the premises for His glory and to change many many lives. Just a few examples. Agatha, a young woman came into the shop who was very ready to accept Christ. She had been seeking Him and just needed a very small amount of understanding about what Jesus did for her on the cross. Once she knew she could be forgiven she took home a little booklet showing her how to accept and make Jesus her Lord, which she did, and later came back to tell the tale of her new found freedom and relationship. Agatha in turn has herself led many to find this wonderful Saviour. A young man on his way to commit suicide received the wonderful news of forgiveness and is walking with Him today, and has a wonderful testimony. There are countless others whose lives will never be the same and only heaven will reveal the full extent of the great love of the One we serve.

Apparent Disaster

While Tom was at work I went with the boys to Church one Sunday morning in 1988, and as I came home and parked the car, I was at first puzzled to find a car sitting outside in a fairly broken up state. As I looked closer I felt the shock as I realized the front of the shop was all smashed up, broken glass, broken glass shelves and the wooden shopfront we had then, all out of place and ill-fitting, looking like it would fall down at the slightest touch. I then panicked and just did not know what to do next. Finally, I telephoned the police and after a little while they came. The police had been called to the accident involving a policeman from another country, who had missed the road, gone over the pavement and ploughed straight into the front of the bookshop smashing everything in its wake. The police left insurance details and I proceeded to get in touch with the insurance company. The surveyor came and examined everything. He was not very reassuring at all and seemed to give me the impression that they may only repair the damage and not necessarily give us a new front and not necessarily replace the broken glass shelves. I was so mystified by that and frankly very scared, so I got to prayer and I heard the Lord give me this scripture. He gave me Exodus 14 v 14. I had no idea what that was until I looked it up.

EXODUS 14:14
The Lord shall fight for you, and ye shall hold your peace.

What an amazing Lord we serve. He is able to communicate to us amidst the panics and stresses of life that we so often face. The outcome took some time. Eventually the insurance company told us that the police were charging the driver with careless driving and immediately the insurance company could not do enough for us. They told us choose any front and any glass shelves we wanted. The amazing thing after all was that we got a front that we really needed and wanted for free. Indeed we serve a wonderful Lord who turns all things around in a marvellous way.

Rodney Howard-Browne, 1995

There are people who come into our lives who profoundly bring change. In December of 1995, Kensington Temple, the church we were attending, invited Rodney Howard-Browne to do a conference in Wembley for a week. I was feeling that I needed to take some time out to spend with the Lord, so I arranged to be able to go every day starting Sunday and ending the following Saturday. I was very excited about this week and was very expectant. Every day I went I saw people being touched all around me but to my chagrin nothing was happening to me, I loved the Lord's presence in the building, but it did not seem to touch me and I was so longing for more from God. As the days went by, Sunday, Monday, Tuesday, Wednesday, nothing seemed to touch me and I was puzzled. As I drove in with a friend on the Thursday I began to share with her that I was disappointed and could not understand what was happening as I was normally very open and easily received a lot of touches from the Lord. In a minute or two my friend began to share a picture she had with me. She said, "I can see that you have what looks like breeze blocks inside you from your middle all the way up to your neck and you are completely blocked up with emotional pain and the Holy Spirit is only able to trickle out of you when He would really like to flow". I must say I did not really like this word and I thought to myself this cannot be true, as I did not feel like this at all. But when I got to the meeting hall I went to a place to be alone with the Lord, and I said I don't get any witness to this, but maybe if it is true will you take this blockage away from me?. The meeting started and still it was just the same, but in the afternoon a change was taking place inside me and as Rodney's wife began to speak and I found myself weeping softly. The leaders of the meeting asked for people who would like to be prayed for to go up to the top of the room and wait. As I moved to that place the presence of the Lord began to get stronger and stronger and next thing, before anybody could get to me to pray for me, I felt like this huge heavy explosion happened inside me as something seemed to fall down on me from above. I just fell to the ground shaking and crying, I sobbed for about 30 minutes and could not stop shaking. I was legless for about three days and could only kneel in coffee queues, or for food, because every time I stood up, I just fell down again. I knew the Lord had done something very deep as I could feel something like a channel had been dug inside me, and that scripture John 7 v 38. *Out of your innermost being shall flow rivers of living water.* I could, for the first time, feel bubbling up from out of my spirit rivers of living water and joy unspeakable. I did not realize that pain that is stored inside could be such a block to His flowing out of us freely. When we are survivors we stuff everything inside to just get through the daily routine. I had become good at stuffing the pain and so I stuffed and stuffed until I was completely full and there was no more room inside. The Holy Spirit seemed to blow up the lot with a large stick of dynamite. That is how it seemed to me, anyhow.

A word in Ireland

As a family we went to Ireland for a holiday. After the week was over, I stayed on for another week. While we were there the first week we went into a Christian Bookshop in Dublin. They were advertising some meetings in the Gresham Hotel in O'Connell Street. The speakers were Andrew Wommack, and Dave Duell. I had never heard of them before. After Tom and the boys went back to London the following Monday morning, I felt the Lord speak to me first thing on that morning, saying to me to get up and go to the Gresham Hotel. This was the last thing I wanted to hear, because I was planning to just chill out and look around the city but the Lord had other ideas. Later on, the Lord would use the teaching I would receive as His plan for the Healing Rooms that would be birthed many years later. His planning in our lives is so amazing and all so timely.

8 *A Personal Word and Three Prophecies About Future Ministry*

The Lord says that "His thoughts are not our thoughts" and how true that is. And "despise not the day of small things". I heard that a group of prophetic people were coming to Luton to encourage the church there with words they heard from the Lord. I was so excited going because I had never been given a personal prophetic word before and was not sure quite what to expect, but I imagined it would run something like, "I have great plans for you" or "this, this and this is going to happen to you, etc. etc."

Well, I got in line for my word and this young teenager came over to me and said "the Lord wants to know you". I was shocked with unbelief, I had travelled a very long way, given up a weekend for this...........

But over the next few weeks, I began to see that the Lord has such a different perspective. Remember, He said there would come a day when people would stand before Him saying they had healed the sick, cast out demons, etc. etc. and He said to them, "depart from me, I NEVER KNEW YOU". Personal relationship with Him is His priority, and He cannot know us personally unless we let

Him into every area of our lives. Now, because He is God, of course He knows everything about us. He is looking for intimacy and that is a two way street. There were three main prophecies that Tom and I were given over the thirty five years since I accepted Jesus into my life. The first one was given to us by a man from the Lewis revival. (The Lewis revival was a sovereign move of repentance over the island in the late forties. People were struck down to the ground with the realization of the awfulness of their sin and where their eternal destination would be if they did not get their lives right with the Lord, and repent. Many saw the glory of the Lord hanging over their houses like every light was on in the middle of the night, and a very strong sense of His presence everywhere). One of the main people the Lord used was a man called Donald.

One of our friends invited Tom and me to a meeting where Donald was speaking. I had no idea who he was or anything about the Lewis revival. When he was finished speaking he came over to Tom and me and he asked if he could pray with us. He said he saw that there would be prayer meetings in our house and that healings would take place. I would love to be able to tell you that I was full of faith about it but I wasn't. I remember laughing to myself wondering how can that be? (Mary the Mother of Jesus said the same thing to the Angel Gabriel when he told her she would give birth to the Messiah). Tom and I both needed so much healing in our own relationship, how could we possibly be used by the Lord to heal anybody else?

1997

Sharon Stone is well known by many as a present day prophet. When we were in Kensington Temple in a meeting where she was the main speaker, she asked Tom and me to stand up and she began to prophesy the following:

The Spirit of God says, "son and daughter, I am looking for those that I could put a scalpel in their hand. I am looking for those who are interested in not just seeing the bodies healed alone, but are interested in seeing the souls restored. I want to put an anointing within the midst of you that helps get people to the cool waters and the refreshing pastures; that their souls might be restored and that they might know a place of strengthening so that they may get on with the battle. I am making you like an oasis in the midst of the desert that others may come and have a cool drink and might be refreshed. You are going to know what it means to touch the tender fragile things of people's heart's. Rise up, Oh Spirit of counsel, rise up, for I have called your mouths to take care of the wounds of others and where others have not been able to cast their cares upon Me. I want to position you in a place where others can do that. You are going to show them how. You are going to be known as a builder of lives. I am going to bring to you Nicodemuses in the night. (Nicodemus came to Jesus in the night secretly). You won't be ones who will have to wonder about how to be advertised, how you are going to grow or how the ministry is going to develop around about you. Word of mouth and testimony will bring forth a new commissioning to you. I saw the doors of your houses opening. These are days of visitation. Even as My Spirit comes in, and as you have allowed Me to ransom you, I am bringing the deliverance of others through you".

Jenny Hockley, 2000

Jenny gave Tom and me at least two very pivotal prophetic words. The first was not such a comfortable word as one would like. She said, "I believe the Lord is saying to you that you are to clean your building from top to bottom, every inch of it and to pray and clean it very thoroughly."

I thought this was a daunting task but nonetheless obedience is better than sacrifice, so we went to an exhibition and purchased a powerful steam cleaner. We started in the attic and cleaned the ceilings, walls, furniture and floors, praying as we went. After six weeks the place was finished. Then the Lord said, "I want you to close down the bookshop for 3 days and do the same cleaning and praying". We put curtains on the windows with a sign that said, 'opening after 3 days'. Also, it meant for us that we had no takings for 3 days and we still had staff to pay and all the usual bills with no takings to pay them. People used to bang on the door and shout, "we know you are in there, let us in." We have always found that when you obey, no matter how inconvenient, God is so faithful because this only happened to us the once. On the fourth day we opened and we took four days takings in one day, so we did not lose a penny. It has never ceased to amaze me how particular the Lord can be. He wanted to clean out this building to make way for His power to move in a way we as yet had no idea of. I believe the next prophecy we would receive was dependent on us obeying the first one.

2nd prophecy by Jenny Hockley, 2001 "rooms of healing"

"I am calling out the broken, I am calling out the wounded, I am calling out those who carry death in their souls. They will come, and they will find healing, they will find peace of mind. You will direct rooms of healing. Oil will flow down the walls of these rooms of healing. The broken will come, the sick will come and find peace in these rooms of healing".

What should we do now with your prophetic words?

We cannot make them happen, but we can prepare. When I was given the word by Jenny Hockley about "rooms of healing", there were no other healing rooms open then. There was no way to copy or see another example of what that could mean. So I read and studied all the scriptures on healing in the Bible. I began to read various books written by people who saw the power of the Lord working in healing. I read the books written about John G. Lake, about his healing ministry and the healing rooms he operated in Spokane and Oregon. John G. Lake, in his lifetime, saw over 100,000 healings take place in the Healing Rooms. So I began to soak myself in healing. I would listen to Andrew Wommack. For me he has some great teaching on healing, and I studied his materials and they were very helpful. Any time anybody came into the bookshop who looked like they would let me pray for them, I would ask them and I saw many people give their lives to Jesus Christ. I saw many people touched by just stepping out and seeing what the Lord would do. As we prepare, the Lord in His time will open the door in the right season. What we can tend to do is, when we don't see anything happen, try to make it happen by kicking the door down. Or we can just give up. There does seem to sometimes be a way that the seed has to die and disappear into the ground altogether, then when we least expect it, up it comes and we seem to step right into it.

Moving out of the bookshop, 1999

The time came, for personal and family reasons. We needed to have a place to live with our family away from the business of the bookshop. We went to look for houses and we found one that we all liked. The couple who lived in it were selling up because of a divorce. The business of this sale was beginning to come to an end and signing a contract would be the next thing to happen. I had a dream one night and in this dream the Lord showed me that we were buying the wrong house. I knew as soon as I woke up that I would have to tell Tom this was the wrong house, and we would have to start to look again. After I peeled Tom off the ceiling we began to look again for houses, and as soon as we stepped into the one we have now, we knew it was the right one for us and we have been very happy in it. I hope we are learning to seek the Lord before making such important decisions.

What is that rod in your hand? 2001

I was sitting in the garden one day feeling a bit low because we had been promised by the Lord that we would enlarge the place of our tent, yet nothing seemed to be happening. I spoke loudly to the Lord, "where is the extension to our property You promised us? "WHERE IS IT?" The Lord seemed to answer me immediately, "what do you have in your hand?" I thought for a while. The only thing I could think of that I had in my hand was the bookshop. We had by this time paid the mortgage off. He said to me, "get an architect to show you what could be done with what you have in your hand". So Tom and I did just that. We made an appointment with the architect and he said that if you knock down four walls you could have quite a big shop. So plans were drawn up and sent in to the council and we found a truly wonderful, skilled builder named Pat Beirne who was a Godsend.

On Boxing Day December 2001, 15 people, friends, relations, and some of the congregation who were from Victory Outreach gathered for the mammoth task of moving every single book and possession from the bookshop to the shop next door, which became vacant for three months. This allowed us time to move out, get the building ready for workmen, walls knocked down, walls re-plastered, new carpets put in, set a re-opened date and move back in and get reopened again. The Lord is so amazing because He speaks to us about every detail if we would only take the time to listen. We had the kitchen and bathroom drawings ready on the night before the bathroom and kitchen were due to start the next day. As I was cleaning up, getting ready for this work to start the next day, I heard the Lord say to me, "you are putting the kitchen and bathroom in the wrong place. It needs to be upstairs not downstairs". Oh no, I thought. How am I going to tell Tom, and then the builder, about the change of plan with so little notice? I have to say, I did not even know if the space was the same or not. So after I peeled Tom off the ceiling again, we rang the builder, who thought for a few minutes, while looking at the plans. He said that would be no problem. What a sigh of relief. If we had not done that, as it has turned out now, we would be short of a bathroom, because we have two on the premises, and, boy, are they both needed, but also downstairs would have been all wrong and it would have been very difficult, probably impossible, to change it all afterwards. A friend said he knew of a bookshop that was closing down which had nice bookstands for sale so Andy Gray got them over to us and off we went.

9 *Finances, Learning to Give and Receive*

Shoes

One of the most valuable lessons the Lord wants us to know is that He is a good Father and loving provider for us in everything. He wants us to know that He even hears our thoughts and He so longs for us to be like Him and learn to hear His voice about the needs all around us, not necessarily just giving our finances to building programmes. But I believe we miss many opportunities to give personal items to somebody who may have a need.

One Sunday morning, as a family, we were on our way to Church and as I was getting ready I was thinking that I would love a new pair of shoes. Raising a family with three boys, their shoes always came first, and of course, with all the playing of "footie", shoes for them did not last long. So mine would be down the list a little way. Anyhow, I was thinking I would love a new leather pair for me. As we were in Church and having coffee afterwards, a lady came up to me and asked me what size shoes I took. It's not the usual question on a Sunday morning over coffee, but when I told her she said that she had bought a new pair of leather shoes yesterday and when she had got them home, she had decided she did not like them so much after all. She related to me that as she was thinking about returning them. The Lord said to her, "give them to Betty Burke". So as she offered me these new shoes in my size I knew of a caring Father, who hears even our thoughts and wants continually to show how He cares. Are we prepared to pay attention to the Lord in the area of finances and let Him become Lord of this difficult area for us to surrender? We like to be in charge or in control, especially in this area. I remember hearing a minister say that if the Lord has your wallet He has everything. In much of the teaching of the Church we can hear teaching about tithing. There are scriptures about tithing, eg. Malachi 3. You and I may feel led to tithe our money to our local church. That may be your main experience of giving. I remember when our boys were small we were tithing on our income. That was for us a huge sacrifice because of our financial difficulties and for anybody with a small income, for instance a single mother raising children, that could mean the cost of meals for her children which would be a much bigger sacrifice than somebody on a very large salary. 10% of a huge income given away will not mean loss of meals for the daily needs of a family. I have often pondered how this can be the correct interpretation of giving when you compare that with the New Testament examples of giving in the early Church (Acts 5).

Instead of taking from the least well off in the congregation they gave where there was need so all were supported financially and had their needs met. The other thing is that if you are open with your finances to the Lord, He will share with you the secrets of people who have needs and will not tell anybody about them, and if you are willing to be the answer to somebody's prayer then you will find yourself first hand seeing a need met. This is one of the most exciting and wonderful experiences there is, I believe. The following are a few examples in my own life. I share these not to lift myself up, but so you can understand that by just putting your 10% in the offering we can miss out on a wonderful trip into the supernatural with the Lord Himself. Remember, Jesus saw the widow putting all she had in the offering. To the eyes of the natural it was not worth noting, but to Him, He saw her giving all she had, and she is in His word forever. The Father hears the cries of His children and He knows all of our needs and the needs of our families. I remember having a dream about a lady who had five children, and all her five children needed shoes. This couple were missionaries in this country and were living by faith, so that meant they were not making their needs known or asking anybody for money or support. They were crying out to their Father in secret. One night, as I slept, I knew this lady had a financial need, but I did not know it by human knowledge but by this dream. I share this not so you will think how good I am, but to show how the Father loves us so much and hears our cries and wants to share His precious children's need with somebody He can trust to fulfill that need. The next morning I telephoned the lady concerned and shared my dream with her. Many tears were shed by both of us as I was so thrilled to hear my Father speaking to me, with the confirmation I received that I was hearing correctly and the sheer delight of being able to meet their need in such a way.

Because we worked in the bookshop full-time holidays were rare and precious. We were often treated to holidays by people who wanted to bless our ministry. Because of lack of time all the boys' school clothes for the year ahead were usually bought in the summer holidays. A day would be taken out for such a task. It was a mammoth task clothing all three boys for the following year. It always worked out that we had enough money for the shopping, but this particular year I did not have any money, so I got to my knees as the holiday came near, and I shared our need this particular morning with the Lord. I did not say a word to Tom, who always looks after the finances, and he does a very good job of it too. I did not want to burden him with this need. I decided to leave it totally to my Father. As the bookshop opened that morning the telephone rang. The accountant was ringing Tom to tell him that I was owed some money for wages that he needed to give me. I was so thrilled at such a quick answer and I got to my knees the next morning to thank the Lord. As I was praying I began to realize that the Lord had another purpose also for that money, as it was a lot more than I needed. Soon a name came to me, the name of a music group who travelled around the world. I knew them by reputation and from selling their CDs, but did not know how to reach them. I eventually found their address and the Lord showed me the amount to give them and I sent the cheque off in the post. After a couple of days I got a call from their leader telling me that on this particular morning he had received a bill for equipment that needed to be repaired and he did not have the money for the repair and was preparing himself for having to tell the team that they would not be leaving for the trip planned because of the situation facing them. The next envelope they received was exactly the amount needed for the repair. As the leader was sharing with me this wonderful news, I was so thrilled to know that I had heard from my Father, who loves all of us so much and wants to show us continually His Fatherly care in His provision for the music group in letting them know He knew their need and had taken care of it before it arrived and for me knowing and experiencing His love for me, in letting me into a secret of one of His children's needs and that I could hear His voice accurately.

Paying the bills

This can be a very "walking on the edge" experience as you never know exactly how much money you are going to have to play with when you are walking by faith in your finances. Our bills for the bookshop usually came all together, and had to be paid at a particular time of the month. By the following Saturday of this particular month we were several thousand short. I was not a little unsettled about it, and kept praying about it, but with no particular answer or insight. During that week Tom and I had been asked to set up a bookstall in a local church for a couple of evenings. During the last evening, after we had been selling for these couple of nights, the pastor got up to read the following passage of Scripture.

2 CORINTHIANS 9 V 6-11 – THE CHEERFUL GIVER

⁶ But this I say: He who sows sparingly will also reap sparingly, and he who sows bountifully will also reap bountifully.

⁷ So let each one give as he purposes in his heart, not grudgingly or of necessity; for God loves a cheerful giver.⁸ And God is able to make all grace abound toward you, that you, always having all sufficiency in all things, may have an abundance for every good work.

⁹ As it is written:
He has dispersed abroad,
He has given to the poor;
His righteousness endures forever."[a]

¹⁰ Now may[b] He who supplies seed to the sower, and bread for food, supply and multiply the seed you have sown and increase the fruits of your righteousness,¹¹ while you are enriched in everything for all liberality, which causes thanksgiving through us to God.

I have to admit that as I heard the pastor begin to read this particular scripture I felt...oh no, some American style pressure to give money and I began to switch off. Instantly I heard the Holy Spirit speak to me with such a strong check (a check or conviction can mean a strong feeling deep inside to pay attention or to do a certain thing) that I needed to pay attention right now, like it was very important. We pray, and the answer often does not come when we expect it, or the way we expect it or in the manner in which we like or would want. When the pastor finished speaking then I heard the Lord say, "I want you to put all the takings from this bookselling event into the offering". I was so indignant, I argued back and forth with the Lord about this, like "how come the money we are putting towards the bill, which is due in a few days now, You are asking me to give away into this offering for church?" Frankly it made no sense whatsoever but, you see, when we know His voice by practising listening and obeying, we learn He always knows best. So I stuffed all the money we had without looking at how much it was into the offering bag and wondered how on earth we were going to manage.

The following Saturday we were so busy in the bookshop, which was rare because it was July and a lot of people are normally away. It was like the people came out of the woodwork from every direction possible and bought large piles of books, Bibles and gifts etc. At the end of the day we were so amazed to find we had enough money to pay everything. Our Father God is so wonderful, His ways are not our ways in any way, shape or form. What a lesson.. PHEW..... so listening to Him is the key.

Pay your vows, 1983

When one of my family members died, we were notified and travelled across to Ireland for the funeral. This family member had left me £1,000. As I was praying about our family, and so much money was wasted on heavy drinking and drunkenness, it seemed to me like nothing of much spiritual value appeared to me to have come from all those years, just so much waste. I went to visit the local parish church close to my home in Dublin, and the minister said to me that he did not think much could ever come from my family or home. This was very painful for me to hear, but I also knew he was probably right. And I began to seek the Lord about this money and I wanted to sow it into souls. So when we met a missionary from India I sowed half this amount of money into his ministry on the streets somewhere in India. Time went by and I forgot about the rest of the money I had vowed to give to the Lord's work. About two years later, I was reading the book of Numbers, chapter 30 where it talks about a person making vows:

NUMBERS 30 v 1-2

Then Moses spoke to the heads of the tribes
concerning the children of Israel, saying, "This is
the thing which the Lord has commanded: ² If a man
makes a vow to the Lord, or swears an oath to bind
himself by some agreement, he shall not break his
word; he shall do according to all that proceeds out of
his mouth.

PSALM 116 v 14

I will pay my vows to the Lord
Now in the presence of all His people.

PSALM 50 v 14

Offer to God thanksgiving,
And pay your vows to the Most High.

Such a spirit of conviction came upon me as I realized that the money (the other half) I had set aside by vow to the Lord had been spent in the changeover from selling tobacco to Christian books that I now needed to give this money into live evangelism. As I was praying, Yvonne, a friend of mine who had stayed with Tom and me overnight, had gone to her car and felt she needed to come and spend the day with me, and I was now able to pray with somebody else as well, so I was able to come to a place of peace when I made a decision to release this money to a ministry with evangelism as its main passion. So, after all, there were seeds coming from my house that were now at work in India and Africa. Only when we go to be with Jesus will we know the results of that obedience. Actually, we reap in this world also. A lady who had been converted to Jesus Christ through one of these ministries in Africa was now living in London. She heard the Lord ask her to come and help us as a volunteer for a season with us. Souls are an eternal investment that will never lose their value. Who knows who will get to heaven because of our obedient sowing and sharing the Gospel? Of course it is never wise to make vows carelessly. They need to be prayerfully thought out.

The original shop

The old shop

Having the bigger shop made

Having a dance with the staff

Later picture of the family

10 *Prayer and Finding Your Place*

When we are in prayer meetings, or conferences, or Sunday services, we can feel in those atmospheres that prayer can be so easy and we can get carried along with the enthusiasm or the feelings we can experience when the Holy Spirit is moving powerfully, and we determine to spend an amount of time every morning with the Lord. When we awake early and get out of a warm bed to spend our determined time or the amount we thought we could, it can for some people be a very different proposition facing that time by oneself, with no goosey feelings, just a cold room. Pushing through this we can find a relationship with the Lord that really pleases us and Him, because we are giving Him our time, which is the most precious commodity we possess. I would recommend starting with a realistic amount of time. According to our schedules it could be morning or evening. Beginning small and consistant is the best and developing it as we grow. It is like any relationship that we begin. It takes time to get to know a friend, to begin to recognize the responses we will get back. Everybody's experience will be different and the way the Lord will relate to you will be different from anybody else. Because we are unique and different from each other, each relationship with the Lord will develop in its own way. Some people are visual, some are sensitive in other areas, and we have to find our own. One of the worst things we can do is to compare ourselves with anybody else in any of our spiritual walk. We could be tempted to think that an intercessor, who may spend hours alone with the Lord praying, is the only way to a successful relationship with the Lord, and if we can't do that then we are a failure. That is a particular calling and therefore there is a special grace or ability for the amount of time spent. Begin where you are and let the Holy Spirit help you (He is the helper after all). He really will, and you find yourself walking closer and closer. We can have shopping lists, the needs of family, friends, church, or our own needs. There is a place of intimacy that we can grow into, where not so many words are flowing but just a sense of His presence, and just being with Him not for what we can get from Him. Couples who have been married for a long time often just sit together and being with one another is enough. Again, do not compare yourself in any way with another. Here is a very important scripture and if we take this scripture on board we will save ourselves a lot of unnecessary heartache.

2 CORINTHIANS 10 v 12

> *For we dare not class ourselves or compare ourselves*
> *with those who commend themselves. But they, measuring*
> *themselves by themselves, and comparing themselves*
> *among themselves, are not wise.*

The Glory of the Lord covers the earth as the waters cover the sea (Habakkuk 2 v 14)

I began to see that the Lord maybe means more with this scripture than I first realized. I always thought it could mean that perhaps revelation knowledge would come down from

above to cover the earth, or a presence that could be felt, and
that may be the case, but I was sensing that the Lord was
showing me that as His body gets more and more filled with
His presence, we release that presence through laying on of
our hands on people, speaking the words we are given to
speak to particular people, witnessing and our very breath is
releasing out of our innermost beings the living water, every
way we can.

JOHN 7 v 38 (AMPLIFIED BIBLE)
He who believes in Me, (who cleaves to and trusts in
and relies on Me) as the Scripture has said. From his
innermost being shall flow (continuously) springs and
rivers of living water.

As I was seeking the Lord about this, somebody gave
me the following picture they felt the Lord had showed
them. They saw a picture of a dandelion flower, when
the flower has died and the fuzzy ball remains (called a
parachute ball), and as I blew on this ball the seeds went
everywhere. I took this as confirmation that one of the
ways we can release the presence of the Lord, as John 7
v 38 says, is by deliberately putting ourselves in a place
where He is able to flow out of us. I remember meeting
a man from Indonesia, who would at every opportunity
shake people's hands, and as he did so, by faith he would
release the presence of the Lord to them. His experience
was that in time many of those people came to faith and
gave their lives to the Lord. The Lord can use even our
eyes when filled with His compassion in order to reach
a person in pain or trouble. This is what the laying on of
hands is, desiring the Lord to flow out from within us as
we touch a person. The Holy Spirit being released out of
our hands, breath or even like Peter in the book of Acts.

ACTS 5 v 14 – 16

*¹⁴ And believers were increasingly added to the Lord,
multitudes of both men and women, ¹⁵ so that they
brought the sick out into the streets and laid them
on beds and couches, that at least the shadow of
Peter passing by might fall on some of them. ¹⁶ Also
a multitude gathered from the surrounding cities
to Jerusalem, bringing sick people and those who
were tormented by unclean spirits, and they were
all healed.*

The Lord is full of creative ideas of how to reach the people
He loves so much, and sent Jesus to die for. Nothing leaves
heaven till something leaves the earth first.

A place called there, the place where you belong

You will flourish when in your place, Divine prosperity
is there.

I KINGS 17 v 1-7 – ELIJAH PROCLAIMS A DROUGHT

*¹ And Elijah the Tishbite, of the inhabitants of Gilead,
said to Ahab, "As the Lord God of Israel lives, before
whom I stand, there shall not be dew nor rain these
years, except at my word."*

*² Then the word of the Lord came to him, saying,³
"Get away from here and turn eastward, and hide by
the Brook Cherith, which flows into the Jordan.⁴ And it
will be that you shall drink from the brook, and I have
commanded the ravens to feed you there."*

*⁵ So he went and did according to the word of the
Lord, for he went and stayed by the Brook Cherith, which
flows into the Jordan.⁶ The ravens brought him bread and*

*meat in the morning, and bread and meat in the evening;
and he drank from the brook.*[7] *And it happened after a
while that the brook dried up, because there had been no
rain in the land.*

I KINGS 17 v 8-16 - ELIJAH AND THE WIDOW

[8] *Then the word of the Lord came to him, saying,*

[9] *"Arise, go to Zarephath, which belongs to Sidon,
and dwell there. See, I have commanded a widow there to
provide for you."*

[10] *So he arose and went to Zarephath. And when he
came to the gate of the city, indeed a widow was there
gathering sticks. And he called to her and said, "Please
bring me a little water in a cup, that I may drink."*

[11] *And as she was going to get it, he called to her and
said, "Please bring me a morsel of bread in your hand."*

[12] *So she said, "As the Lord your God lives, I do not
have bread, only a handful of flour in a bin, and a little
oil in a jar; and see, I am gathering a couple of sticks
that I may go in and prepare it for myself and my son,
that we may eat it, and die."*

[13] *And Elijah said to her, "Do not fear; go and do as
you have said, but make me a small cake from it first, and
bring it to me; and afterward make some for yourself and
your son.*

[14] *For thus says the Lord God of Israel: 'The bin of
flour shall not be used up, nor shall the jar of oil run dry,
until the day the Lord sends rain on the earth.'"*

[15] *So she went away and did according to the word of
Elijah; and she and he and her household ate for many
days.* [16] *The bin of flour was not used up, nor did the jar
of oil run dry, according to the word of the Lord which
He spoke by Elijah.*

MATTHEW 4 V 19

And he (Jesus) said unto them, Follow me, and I will
make you fishers of men.

Never stay when you know the season is over, when He has
directed you to the next place. Move on when He says to
move on, no matter what anybody tells you. The Lord does
not do everything the same all the way through your life,
because you will just repeat and repeat, or do what you did
last time, and not seek for new direction. We tend not to
want to find out from the Lord the way to deal with the latest
test. There can never be a testimony without a test. If you
take the 'test' out of 'testimonies', all you are left with is the
'monies', ie, complaints or moaning.

11 *Shame and What Can Come Down and Hit You*

Shame is a very big deal for many of us. We carry shame even if we are not aware of it. Further on in this chapter I will share with you my own testimony of being set free from the shame of illegitimacy. Any way in which we are singled out that is negative can cause us to carry shame. For example, divorce, failure of any kind, bankruptcy, rejection, sickness, too much weight, too little weight, physical scars, poverty, adoption, abortion, barrenness, height challenges. We can wear shame like a cloak.

The wonderful thing about the Lord is that He takes the shame and destroys it at the cross. He hung there for us, taking our place. To hang on a cross was ultimate shame. He hung there naked for all to see and despise. He did all this for us so we do not have to carry it. He wants that cloak removed for good.

ISAIAH 61:6-8 (AMPLIFIED BIBLE)
⁶But you shall be called the priests of the Lord; people will speak of you as the ministers of our God. You shall eat the wealth of the nations, and the glory [once that of your captors] shall be yours.⁽ᴬ⁾⁷Instead of your [former] shame you shall have a twofold recompense; instead of

*dishonour and reproach [your people] shall rejoice in
their portion. Therefore in their land they shall possess
double [what they had forfeited]; everlasting joy shall
be theirs.*

*[8]For I the Lord love justice; I hate robbery and wrong
with violence or a burnt offering. And I will faithfully
give them their recompense in truth, and I will make an
everlasting covenant or league with them.*

There are many people the Lord shows us in Scripture
He lifted up who would otherwise be despised or passed
over. Here are some examples: Ruth was a Moabite and
according to Deuteronomy 23 v 3 a Moabite could not
enter the assembly or worship. You can read her story in
the book of Ruth. But because she married Boaz, together
they had a son called Obed, who in turn had a son called
Jesse, who was the father of king David. Therefore
Ruth actually got into the genealogy of Jesus Christ. So
we can see that Ruth was lifted up to an amazing place
of honour.

MATTHEW 1 v 1-6

*[1] This is a record of the ancestors of Jesus the Messiah, a
descendant of David[a] and of Abraham:*
[2] Abraham was the father of Isaac.
*Isaac was the father of Jacob. Jacob was the father of
Judah and his brothers.*
*[3] Judah was the father of Perez and Zerah (whose mother
was Tamar).*
Perez was the father of Hezron.
Hezron was the father of Ram.[b]
[4] Ram was the father of Amminadab.
Amminadab was the father of Nahshon.

Nahshon was the father of Salmon.
⁵ Salmon was the father of Boaz (whose mother
was Rahab).
Boaz was the father of Obed (whose mother was Ruth).
Obed was the father of Jesse.
⁶ Jesse was the father of King David.
David was the father of Solomon (whose mother was
Bathsheba, the widow of Uriah).

Another example is:

I CHRONICLES 2 v 4
Tamar, Judah's daughter-in-law, gave birth to Judah's
sons Perez and Zerah. Judah had five sons in all.

Perez was not born from a conventional marriage. He
will have come from a union that was very deceptive and
incestuous. A very shameful situation. The Lord redeemed
this whole situation by putting Perez in the genealogy of
Jesus Christ, which again is such a huge honour. Most
significantly, through the ancestry of Tamar and Perez,
the Messianic line continued, culminating with Jesus
Christ Himself.

LUKE 3 v 31-33
Nathan was the son of David.
³² David was the son of Jesse.
Jesse was the son of Obed.
Obed was the son of Boaz.
Boaz was the son of Salmon.[h]
Salmon was the son of Nahshon.
³³ Nahshon was the son of Amminadab.
Amminadab was the son of Admin.
Admin was the son of Arni.[i]

Arni was the son of Hezron.
Hezron was the son of Perez.

My Whirlwind, 1982

The curse of illegitimacy

DEUTERONOMY 23 v 2
> *Regulations concerning Worship*
> *If a person is illegitimate by birth, neither he nor his*
> *descendants for ten generations may be admitted to the*
> *assembly of the LORD.*

It can be difficult to understand why the verses in this passage are in Scripture but this is where we just trust the Lord, and that He has His reasons, but of course after Jesus Christ came He made a way for us to be set free from all the consequences of shame and these verses. Being born illegitimate is quite a big deal. People don't always understand that spiritually it really matters how your parents were, and the state in which they were when you were conceived. I was born from an adulterous relationship. That leaves a child open and unprotected from unclean behaviour. As I look back I realize the enemy was trying every way he could to get me into immorality, pornography and every other kind of sexual deviancy. When I was a child there was abuse of every kind around, shouting, uncleanness of many kinds, sexual abuse, the dread of somebody coming into the house drunk, which would probably end up with the police being called from across the road and somebody being removed by force. Illegitimacy can lead to an unnatural obsession with sexuality. Fortunately I was born into a conservative society and there were not any shows or films released in Ireland of an explicit sexual nature at that time, quite unlike the present time. So there was some protection in place for me. When I became born again, having given my life to Jesus Christ, the real battle began, most of which I was unable to do much about. I would be minding my own business looking after the children, cooking, cleaning, doing household chores and serving in the bookshop and it was like something would come upon me that I could not stop. It seemed to come down and cover my head and shoulders, and there would come pictures, film shows of the mind, words that were terrible, horrible black feelings and I thought I would end up needing hospitalization for the mentally unbalanced, so I was terrified to tell anybody of the terror I felt. This would come several times during the day, and especially at times of worship. I remember having to leave the communion service to vomit in the bathroom. I would feel faint and passed out a few times. I was tormented. Now not everybody who is born outside marriage may have those symptoms or experiences, but there may be temptations to be promiscuous at the least, with the same scenario of having a child outside of marriage and so the curse goes on and reproduces again and again until somebody breaks through and stops this going down the family line by bringing this curse to the feet of Jesus who carried all our curses at the cross of Calvary.

However, for me there was more of the same for about six months. I began to cry out to the Lord more and more. The thing was that I thought this was me, and I was the cause of the thoughts and pictures, I did not want them but they still came more and more regularly. I was praying one day and I said to the Lord, "You have to do something about this because I can no longer go on carrying this any more." I did not even tell Tom because I did not want to have to leave my children and go into a mental hospital, maybe for good, I believed at that time. There must be something terrible wrong with me to be like this.

As I was reading the Bible that day light began to dawn at last. I was reading the story of Gehazi (the servant of Elijah the Prophet of Israel) and something about this passage really spoke to me. I was not sure exactly what yet, but was about to find out shortly (2 Kings 5 v 1-27, New King James Version).

Naaman's Leprosy Healed

¹ Now Naaman, commander of the army of the king of Syria, was a great and honorable man in the eyes of his master, because by him the LORD had given victory to Syria. He was also a mighty man of valor, but a leper. ² And the Syrians had gone out on raids, and had brought back captive a young girl from the land of Israel. She waited on Naaman's wife. ³ Then she said to her mistress, "If only my master were with the prophet who is in Samaria! For he would heal him of his leprosy." ⁴ And Naaman went in and told his master, saying, "Thus and thus said the girl who is from the land of Israel."

⁵ Then the king of Syria said, "Go now, and I will send a letter to the king of Israel."
So he departed and took with him ten talents of silver, six thousand shekels of gold, and ten changes of clothing.
⁶ Then he brought the letter to the king of Israel, which said, Now be advised, when this letter comes to you, that I have sent Naaman my servant to you, that you may heal him of his leprosy. ⁷ And it happened, when the king of Israel read the letter, that he tore his clothes and said, "Am I God, to kill and make alive, that this man sends a man to me to heal him of his leprosy? Therefore please consider, and see how he seeks a quarrel with me."

⁸ So it was, when Elisha the man of God heard that the king of Israel had torn his clothes, that he sent to the

king, saying, "Why have you torn your clothes? Please
let him come to me, and he shall know that there is a
prophet in Israel."

⁹ Then Naaman went with his horses and chariot, and
he stood at the door of Elisha's house. ¹⁰ And Elisha sent
a messenger to him, saying, "Go and wash in the Jordan
seven times, and your flesh shall be restored to you, and
you shall be clean." ¹¹ But Naaman became furious,
and went away and said, "Indeed, I said to myself, 'He
will surely come out to me, and stand and call on the
name of the Lᴏʀᴅ his God, and wave his hand over the
place, and heal the leprosy.' ¹² Are not the Abanah[a]
and the Pharpar, the rivers of Damascus, better than all
the waters of Israel? Could I not wash in them and be
clean?" So he turned and went away in a rage. ¹³ And
his servants came near and spoke to him, and said, "My
father, if the prophet had told you to do something great,
would you not have done it? How much more then, when
he says to you, 'Wash, and be clean'?" ¹⁴ So he went
down and dipped seven times in the Jordan, according to
the saying of the man of God; and his flesh was restored
like the flesh of a little child, and he was clean.

¹⁵ And he returned to the man of God, he and all
his aides, and came and stood before him; and he said,
"Indeed, now I know that there is no God in all the earth,
except in Israel; now therefore, please take a gift from
your servant."

¹⁶ But he said, "As the Lᴏʀᴅ lives, before whom I
stand, I will receive nothing." And he urged him to take
it, but he refused.

¹⁷ So Naaman said, "Then, if not, please let your
servant be given two mule-loads of earth; for your
servant will no longer offer either burnt offering or
sacrifice to other gods, but to the Lᴏʀᴅ. ¹⁸ Yet in this thing

*may the LORD pardon your servant: when my master goes
into the temple of Rimmon to worship there, and he leans
on my hand, and I bow down in the temple of Rimmon—
when I bow down in the temple of Rimmon, may the LORD
please pardon your servant in this thing."*

*¹⁹ Then he said to him, "Go in peace." So he
departed from him a short distance.*

Gehazi's Greed

*²⁰ But Gehazi, the servant of Elisha the man of God, said,
"Look, my master has spared Naaman this Syrian, while
not receiving from his hands what he brought; but as the
LORD lives, I will run after him and take something from
him." ²¹ So Gehazi pursued Naaman. When ³⁹ Naaman
saw him running after him, he got down from the chariot
to meet him, and said, "Is all well?"*

*²² And he said, "All is well. My master has sent me,
saying, 'Indeed, just now two young men of the sons of
the prophets have come to me from the mountains of
Ephraim. Please give them a talent of silver and two
changes of garments.'"*

*²³ So Naaman said, "Please, take two talents." And
he urged him, and bound two talents of silver in two
bags, with two changes of garments, and handed them to
two of his servants; and they carried them on ahead of
him. ²⁴ When he came to the citadel, he took them from
their hand, and stored them away in the house; then he
let the men go, and they departed. ²⁵ Now he went in
and stood before his master. Elisha said to him, "Where
did you go, Gehazi?" And he said, "Your servant did not
go anywhere."*

*²⁶ Then he said to him, "Did not my heart go with you
when the man turned back from his chariot to meet you?
Is it time to receive money and to receive clothing, olive*

groves and vineyards, sheep and oxen, male and female
servants? [27] *Therefore the leprosy of Naaman shall cling*
to you and your descendants forever." And he went out
from his presence leprous, as white as snow.

That day my pastor heard the Lord telling him to come and
visit me. As he came into the bookshop and through into
the kitchen, he just stood there looking at me. It was like a
revelation that hit me and I just knew I was fighting an evil
spirit, and that it was not coming from me but was coming
at me and upon me, being sent to harass me by the enemy.
I felt the wonderful joy as I began to realize that I could
fight this thing off from me in the wonderful name of Jesus
Christ of Nazereth. My pastor told me that he believed the
Lord was showing him that there was a curse on my life
that needed to be broken and that he had been listening
to Derek Prince on a cassette tape and that the following
week on a Tuesday evening the church would sit around
and listen to the tape and see what the Lord would do. We
listened to the tape as Derek Prince explained to us that
curses still operate today on us and that we need to deal
with them by bringing to bear on these curses all the Cross
has accomplished for us.

Biblical explanation of curses

The Lord was showing me the battles we face on a day to
day basis CAN be the results of agreements that we or our
ancestors have made with the enemy. Thank God, we can
renounce (means to speak off) them from off ourselves.

2 CORINTHIANS 4 V 2 (AMPLIFIED BIBLE)
We have renounced disgraceful ways (secret thoughts,
feelings, desires and underhandedness, the methods

*and arts that men hide through shame); we refuse to
deal craftily (to practice trickery and cunning) or to
adulterate or handle dishonestly the word of God.*

Curses begin in the Bible in Genesis.

Genesis 3:16-18 (New King James Version)
*16 To the woman He said:
"I will greatly multiply your sorrow and your conception;
In pain you shall bring forth children;
Your desire shall be for your husband,
And he shall rule over you."
17 Then to Adam He said, "Because you have heeded the
voice of your wife, and have eaten from the tree of which
I commanded you, saying, 'You shall not eat of it':
"Cursed is the ground for your sake;
In toil you shall eat of it
All the days of your life. 18 Both thorns and thistles it
shall bring forth for you,
And you shall eat the herb of the field.*

Throughout Scripture there are many examples of curses in
operation, but the wonderful news is the following scripture
in the New Testament.

Galatians 3 v 13
*Christ has redeemed us from the curse of the law, having
become a curse for us (for it is written, "Cursed is
everyone who hangs on a tree").*

As we were listening to the cassette there was a prayer we
could join in with the speaker of renouncing and repenting,
putting any curses we may be under on the Cross. As I was
joining in that prayer, I began to notice a whirlwind begin

to gather around me. I could feel the strength of the wind and I knew the Lord was setting me free that moment. I was so intoxicated with the wonderful presence of the Lord, I could not stand to my feet for about thirty minutes. I knew a great change had come into my life. I knew I could win this battle with the thoughts coming into my mind. I began to have a great victory in that area. Immediately the temptation or unclean thought would come, I would rebuke it and these pictures, thoughts and feelings would disappear instantly. Eventually they did not come any more, because the enemy knew he had lost that particular battle now that the curse was broken off from me and I was free.

The blood of Jesus Christ still works in our lives today and the Cross is still setting people free. This analogy makes it easy to understand. A large supermarket has enough washing powder on its shelves to wash the clothes of all the area around the supermarket. We have dirty clothes and linen that needs washing. If we do not take the washing powder and put it in with the clothes in the washing machine they will remain dirty. Similarly we have a choice whether to appropriate all the Cross of Jesus Christ has accomplished for us or not. I want it all.

Getting set free from the spirit of fear, 1988

I had fear, because of the experiences of childhood, although there were many good ones. My grandmother was a wonderful woman. Having been left a widow at a young age, and having to raise three children alone was not an easy task. In Ireland in the 1930's and 1940's there were not weekly benefits available like there are today, so she had many financial struggles, but she always said how she would pray and trust the Lord and there was always food and clothes. Unfortunately, all her children were affected by alcoholism in some way, some more than others. So there was a lot of fear around, fear about somebody coming in drunk and what the results of each episode would be.

I always knew I carried fears. When I would sit in church, I preferred the back and did not like anybody looking or staring at me. In the church where we were worshipping there were two musicians, and I also played the guitar. When the pastor, Stephen, who was one of those musicians, had a sabbatical, the second guitarist left, so there was nobody to lead the worship for the next six Sundays but me. The fear and trepidation was indescribable, because even though I was very afraid I also knew that whatever the cost we need to obey the Lord, and I knew this would be a time of growth for me. The Lord's timing is so amazing because just before I was supposed to start the six weeks worship leading I was invited to a nearby meeting, which took place on a Tuesday evening. As I went to this meeting I kept having these ideas not to go. It was a very strong pull not to go, and I swayed a bit back and forth, then I decided I was going anyway. The man who was speaking that night was Phil Edwards and he was speaking on being delivered from demons. As soon as he started to speak the fear in me began to manifest in earnest and I noticed my stomach area full of butterflies and was very uncomfortable, and I knew this fear was now a spirit and I needed to get rid of it. As Phil came to the end of the message he asked people who wanted prayer to put their hand up. I instantly put my hand up and Phil came over to me and took me aside a little and began to pray for me. He asked me how I was feeling and I said I could feel the centre of my being very uncomfortable. He began to command the spirit of fear to leave, and then he would ask where the feeling was now, and I said it had moved to my chest area. Then Phil prayed again and he asked me, "where is it now?" and I remember feeling it move to my throat. He prayed again and as he did I knew this spirit left me, and I was free. The subsequent fruit of that ministry was that I now was much more comfortable being at the front and being stared at was not so important, as self-consciousness faded into the background. The fruit of all that we do and happens to us has to be a changing experience, a more evident walk with Jesus, otherwise there is no point and it is just time-wasting for everybody concerned. Jesus says in Scripture to look for the fruit.

MATTHEW 7 v 20
Therefore by their fruits you will know them.

That was such a turning point in my walk with the Lord and crucial for the calling and destiny on my life. Fear is very common in us and it may not always be a demon spirit, but it can stem from a circumstance in our childhood and a demon attaches itself on to it to make it so much stronger.

Two other fears that I had were fast cars and flying, particularly the drops during turbulence. I have flown to many countries and it was a very difficult experience for me, but I would never give up. Joyce Meyer has this brilliant expression, "do it afraid anyway". There is often a reason for fears and it helps with gaining our freedom to know where the fear has come from. I was having dinner with a prophet friend of mine and we were planning to go to Australia on a ministry trip. This was such an exciting thing for me, but I knew it would be over 24 hours of flying each way. As I began to share my fear with my friend, she said I think I know what the root of this fear is. "Oh, good" I said, "when can we deal with it?", so we made an appointment to meet again in a few weeks. As we prayed a few weeks later, the Holy Spirit came very close to me in a very comforting way and I was taken back in time. I realized I was inside my mother's tummy, and I found myself being taken up a hill very fast. I could sense the green grass rushing by and I was speeded up that hill. We came to the top and a cement ledge. Next thing I was being dropped and my mother was jumping, trying to have a miscarriage. As she reached the bottom there was Jesus catching me and saying, "I would not let this happen to you, because you are mine". Some of you reading this may think this is crazy, but all I can tell you that is what happened and I now knew what the reason was for hating the dropping in the air as the aeroplane hit turbulence. I believe the Lord was showing me that some of the fears we have are rooted in real events. When I fly now it's much easier than it once was.

He wants the cloak of shame removed for good. As we or our ancestors may have made agreements with the enemy, these agreements can affect us today, and they may be the reason for some of the battles we face on a day-to-day basis. It is a good idea to have 'generational deliverence' or 'restoring the foundations ministry' to help us renounce and break these agreements. They can be placed at the foot of the cross where they belong, no longer to have the same effect on our lives.

Women's Aglow, 1993-2001

This period of my life was a great season. While at Kensington Temple I remember Colin Dye teaching on the following scripture:

1 KINGS 19 v 19-21 (NEW KING JAMES VERSION)
Elisha Follows Elijah
   [19] *So he departed from there, and found Elisha the son of Shaphat, who was plowing with twelve yoke of oxen before him, and he was with the twelfth. Then Elijah*

*passed by him and threw his mantle on him. [20] And he
left the oxen and ran after Elijah, and said, "Please
let me kiss my father and my mother, and then I will
follow you."*

*And he said to him, "Go back again, for what have I
done to you?"*

*[21] So Elisha turned back from him, and took a yoke of
oxen and slaughtered them and boiled their flesh, using
the oxen's equipment, and gave it to the people, and they
ate. Then he arose and followed Elijah, and became
his servant.*

Elisha, who was involved in a particular task of ploughing,
had to lay it down before moving on to the next part of his
destiny. As I heard this teaching I knew the Lord was asking
me to lay down what I was doing, i.e. worship leading. In
fact, I felt I had to give away my guitar and music and all
the extras with that ministry. It was very painful for me to do
that as I had been given that guitar, it had a beautiful tone,
and I loved it. But the Lord was requiring it of me and I had
no option but to obey. We can miss out if we try to keep
what He wants us to let go of because the next thing we are
going to learn is the next piece in the jigsaw and the whole
puzzle is held up if we don't co-operate. I don't believe the
Lord necessarily always makes us be obedient, but we are
showing lack of trust and the thing we hold onto can become
dust in our hands if we do not let it go, and that is much more
painful in the end. As I moved on, the next thing happened
after about six months, when the worship leading was finally
dead. I was invited to join Women's Aglow. A new chapter
was opening in Leyton, and I was asked to be the Vice-
President. The lady, Elva, who asked me, was a dear friend,
who in fact had bought the first Christian book I ever put in
the window. I knew immediately that this was the Lord, and

so began a whole new learning of skills, leadership, learning
to follow the Holy Spirit, learning to work with Christians
from other denominations. Now my judgemental attitude
had to be challenged again as I had to work with Christians
who worshipped in ways I was not fond of or did not believe
all the things I believed in. This was challenging indeed. But
I found out that Jesus wants us all to be one. That does not
mean we have to agree on everything but we can lay our
differences down for the greater thing which is to spread the
gospel of the kingdom further together without necessarily
building up our own particular group of believers but the
Church in general. He loves His own body, and as the
scripture teaches, which part of the body can I say I don't
need, or which part of the body cannot teach me anything?
Am I too proud to only learn from people who agree with
me on everything? I believe we learn from sharing with each
other. We begin to see the bigger picture. As I was now in
Aglow I was being stretched and stretched. I remember once
that the speaker booked for the evening cancelled and Elva
rang me up with a few hours notice as she felt the Lord say,
ask Betty. I had no option but to step in as I had an inner
witness (feeling in my gut). I was so nervous, I remember,
knowing that I had to speak for about 40 minutes or so. I
remember continually looking at the clock thinking, five
minutes gone, then ten, then twenty now only twenty to go.
When on a visit to America to a Women's Aglow conference,
I stayed with a lady who was a prophet. One day, while in
her house, she picked up my Bible and put it into my hands
and said to me, "you sell it, now you are going to preach
it." I felt immediately a desire come into me to do just that.
Remember, from earlier in my story, I had every fear going,
I was still working on people looking at me from the front,
especially as Aglow got larger and larger. Instantly the
thoughts of preaching the Word was a desire for me and I

looked forward to that with great excitement. One of the regional presidents was Margaret Derrick. I asked her if any chapters needed speakers would she consider asking me? This wonderful lady took a risk and booked me in for some meetings. And so began my training for preaching, learning as I went. The time came for the next piece of the jigsaw. After three years it was time for Elva to move on from Aglow and so the presidency became vacant. I was eventually asked to consider this role. I had the conviction that leadership is a very serious business, and not at all about having a title, or advantage, but a responsibility that one day I would have to give an account for. I felt that the Lord would have to let me know personally if this was what He wanted, as I would not take the role otherwise.

MOSES HAD A CONVERSATION WITH THE LORD ONE DAY IN EXODUS 33 v 14-15

> *[14]And the Lord said, My Presence shall go with you, and I will give you rest.[15]And Moses said to the Lord, If Your Presence does not go with me, do not carry us up from here!*

I did not want to be leading anything if He did not call me and let me know He was calling me. When I was invited to take this role, I said to the leaders, "I will pray and let you know whether He says yes or no." Several people said to me, "we know it is you and of course you should take this role up", and maybe there can be a pressure on us when this is happening, but I knew I had to resist this because I needed to know for myself. It is all very well when everything is going well, but when you hit the problems that always come with leadership, one needs to know that He has called you, so the anointing of wisdom is there for the call and all the other gifts that are needed. You know He is there for you in

a special way and will see you through every difficulty that
you will have to face. I have observed leaders that were not
so sure of His calling. When trouble and discouragement hit,
the temptation to walk away was harder to overcome. After
two months I still had heard nothing, and I received several
phone calls for an answer from the leaders. I wouldn't blame
them for being fed up with me, but I still could not step into
that role until I was sure He had spoken to me. He was also
testing me to see if I would bow to opinion or wait for Him.
I was given a date by which I had to say yes or no. This
was a Saturday morning, I remember. We used to sing and
worship on these Saturday mornings and I remember saying
to the Lord, "today is the day and I have to let them know
by 11.00am today". As I worshipped He said to me "this is
Me. Take up this role". With joy I jumped up and down and
those who know me well know what that means. Everybody
can tell when I am excited and so I relayed my answer. The
next three years were such a blessing. We saw many lives
changed, many come to know Jesus as their Lord and be
born again. Many received physical and emotional healing.
Many received spiritual gifts such as tongues and prophetic
utterances. This is one of the ways in which I saw how the
Lord loves faithfulness. One of the ladies who came regularly
to Aglow asked if she could bring the flowers for the table
every time and I was so thrilled to say yes. Eventually she
began to move more and more in the Spirit, she began to sing
and play the keyboard prophetically and I know she will be
used more and more in her giftings. It began with a simple
serving and moved on to a higher calling. The Lord loves
faithfulness and He rewards it well. After three years, sadly
my time came to an end, and I had to lay down yet another
thing He had given me. It was time for the next piece in
the jigsaw and my training in this area was over. So, thank
you, Women's Aglow for all your wonderful leadership. It

was such a blessing and was invaluable for me. I would recommend this to any woman, because she will be mightily blessed if she enters with a heart to serve.

Listen to a teaching by Andrew Wommack

One day as I was listening to Andrew, he began to speak about John. G. Lake, and how the original healing rooms that John G. Lake had in the 1920's in Spokane, Washington, were re-opening after eighty years. I was unaware of this. We had planned to go to America that year on business for the bookshop and as I listened to Andrew speaking I became aware that we were going to the West Coast of America, which is the same side as Spokane, Washington. I telephoned immediately and found that the very weekend we would be there was the weekend they had a training course. So we booked right away. Little did we know that the events of the next few months would change our lives completely.

12 *Visiting Spokane and Opening Healing Rooms, July 2002*

We flew out to America in such warfare, with so many things trying to stop us going. That could be a pointer that somebody does not want you to go, because your destiny can lie in a particular obedience. We arrived in Spokane, Washington. We saw the place where John. G. Lake had his original healing rooms. We went to where the healing rooms are now located and I have to say that as I entered that building I could sense the presence of the Holy Spirit, so tangible was His anointing. I had always wanted our bookshop to feel like that to people who entered. I remember thinking this is what I want for us in Leyton, London. We started the 3 day training and on the last day was the impartation, which meant that the leaders went around and anointed everybody for healing. The Holy Spirit was very strongly on me, and I was completely blitzed. We had prophecies about our bookshop being filled up with water to the very top and then flowing out all over the nation. I don't think any place has ever affected me more. I cried so much in the airport and on the flight back. I never wanted to leave. When we got back armed with books and materials all about healing rooms and how to start, now the rubber was about to hit the road. I was faced with what to do with this impartation. I knew that it's not just about getting blasted with the Holy Spirit, perhaps rolling around the floor, or laughing. I was given a commission and now it was time to get down to business. The Lord gave me the names of two ladies and I made phone-calls to them to talk to them.

An amazing thing happened a little while later. A man called Trevor came into the bookshop asking for me. As I went to meet him, I slightly recognized him, but did not know his name. The remarkable thing about him was he could not speak, only shake, and I immediately knew where he had been. Trevor and his wife Barbara went to Spokane after us to a Healing Rooms conference in September 2002, and they were given our name and address so we could connect with each other. Trevor and Barbra felt they should start Healing Rooms also, so we decided to make a date to start training that following November with the other two names and a few more that the Lord would show me. Sometimes I would meet people in the bookshop or would see them buying books on healing and I would invite them to a training course. So eight of us began that November of 2002. We showed the videos of the training we had done and week by week we went though the course. Each evening we would pray for the others and see the Holy Spirit move in power. This all happened in the bookshop when the shop was closed as a trainee doctor and his wife were living upstairs. Tom and I had moved out by then and were living in our house.

At the end of the six weeks training I was puzzled as to what to do next. There were no other healing rooms operating in England then, no model to follow in this country, not sure what I was doing, I was so dependant on the Holy Spirit to show me what to do next. When we got to the place of the training being over, He said "I want you to practice on each other". So we did that for a while, and then we had another training. That meant we had another eight to practice on. Then one more training made us about 20 team members. Then I was wondering what we should do about opening rooms up. As we were using the bookshop floor, books were all around and there was one called "40 days" that seemed to stand out and after working it out that would be April 7th 2003.

We had let out the flat upstairs to a young man, called Mark, who was training to be a doctor. We had promised him and his wife that we would let them stay there until he was qualified. That meant three years in total. We had this dilemma that we needed the rooms for the healing rooms yet we had promised him and his wife the three years. So we got to prayer. A friend that we had not seen for five years came in one day, because he said the Lord told him to. He needed somebody to run a Christian house up the road, and there was a very nice flat going at a reasonable rent. Did I know anybody? With tears streaming down my face, I said I did and we put Stewart and Mark together and he and Donna moved out the next week. Truly what a great faithful God we serve.

Opening healing rooms

The forty days were up and we opened on Monday morning the 7th of April 2003, and a Wednesday evening to begin with. We soon began to keep on training and training. Some people came onto the team for a season and would move on to the next assignment in their lives. We have a lot of the original team with us still. We have about thirty churches represented and many nations also. I still pinch myself today, as I cannot believe how blessed

I am to see the Lord moving so powerfully on the teams and on the clients. I have seen people come on the team and grow so fast. Their gifts become apparent as they take steps to move out into the gifts that often lie dormant on the inside of us, not getting used very often. The Healing Rooms are like a greenhouse. Everything grows quickly with practice.

Learning to practice

HEBREWS 5 v 14

> [14]But solid food is for full-grown men, for those whose senses and mental faculties are trained by practice to discriminate and distinguish between what is morally good and noble and what is evil and contrary either to divine or human law.

We learnt to minister by practising, making mistakes, getting up and going on to try again.

We learn to recognize what the Lord means and the different ways He makes His ways known. We get to know when angels are around by sensing their presence, as they are very involved in ministry. We learn by practice to allow our spirit to come to the front and become more important than we have before. The disciples learnt by practice, so will we.

We have many testimonies of people coming into the bookshop and feeling the presence of the Lord, and even being healed without anybody touching them.

Customers from time to time come and tell us that when they walk in the bookshop they can sense the presence of the Lord. Some have testified having come in feeling sick, and after a short time begin to notice the sickness leaving. Even some have found it difficult to stay on their feet. Praise the Lord.

2nd expansion 2005 and the Lord standing at the photocopier

I was given a word from the Lord by a customer in the bookshop one day, "You will expand again". Well, the Lord has always dealt with me in this way, that we get a space and when it is full we get more. We were full everywhere, it did not seem there was anywhere else to go to expand. Then Barbara, who now directs the Thurrock Healing Rooms, gave me a catalogue with chalets on the front, and said "you will need this". I must admit I sort of put it aside, thinking "I can't see how this could be of any use to us."

Adjoining our building at the back was a spare piece of land with a tree on it. This tree would shed seeds around May time and was very annoying indeed. The council came to prune it back a few times and at this particular time it seemed like it was about to split in two and fall down. So I did what I would normally do and got in touch with the local council again in order for them to come and cut it down. They wrote and replied that they were not liable to deal with the tree, as it was not on council land. I asked whose land it was, and they said only the Land Registry knew. So we got in touch with the Land Registry and they said nobody owned it. It was a piece of land where we would store various things from time to time, so we would park the car, etc. etc. We fenced it off and it was added to our property by the Land Registry. At this stage we were given two gifts of money to have the large tree removed. Then we got our wonderful builder Patrick on the job. He and I were discussing the cementing of the ground and the chalets in the office and my eyes were opened and I saw the Lord standing at the photocopier listening to us. I never cease to be amazed that the creator of the immense universe was interested in this tiny piece of land and some wooden chalets. But He is interested and He watches over His Word to perform it. Patrick cemented the ground over and we bought the famous chalets and, putting them on the newly cemented ground, we use them as prayer rooms.

In the two main prayer rooms upstairs, one of the team felt the Lord say, "this dividing wall needs to be removed". I have to say, Jackie and Steve (who are directors also) like me, were a bit puzzled by this word, because why would you want to remove a wall separating two rooms? Then we were invited to France to train some Healing Rooms there. Our healing rooms were given a gift as a result of this trip. Then we realized that the wall coming down and double doors being put in its place would give us more flexibility for these two rooms and it was much needed. So the money from France paid for that work to be done.

Experiencing healings and miracles, words from the Lord at the healing rooms

I believe there is a difference between healings and miracles. I believe miracles are instant and healings may take place over a period of time. We have seen so many of each. Be grateful for the small things the Lord does. Testify to them and He will give you more.

When the client comes into the healing rooms the first thing that happens is they are given a simple form to fill in, one page only with a few questions on it and the reason for coming for prayer. Then the sheet is taken to the healing room which will have 3 members of the team in it. They will each hold the sheet and ask the Lord what He wants to do in this particular session. Often the sheet is held upside-down so we cannot see what the prayer request is. So there is no influence from what is on the sheet. After a few minutes what the Lord has given is discussed among the team and then they call the client into the room. On one of these occasions a word was given to one of the team, e.g. "Picture frame". (not the real word). Also, they were given a very personal almost directional word after that. The team would have had no idea what the significance of the word was. But they asked the client if the word "picture frame" meant anything to them. The client was stunned because the word was his password for everything, so we had the client's attention and he was ready for the next word the Lord had for him, and was able to receive it very well.

A condition called temporomandibular joint (TMJ)

A young man came down from the North for prayer at the rooms. He had difficulty with his jaw, and had pain, which meant he could not sleep easily or chew food. I talked to this man at the door on the way out and it was apparent from the conversation that he was a little disappointed as it seemed to him that he was going home the same way he came. I met this man six months later and he shared with me how a few days later he decided to believe the promises of the Lord for healing, and after a few days he noticed that the pain was gone and he could now eat and move his jaw around normally with sleep restored.

Healing a lady with frozen shoulder

We were praying in a team for a lady who could only get her arm up to about half way and after prayer there was no apparent change in her condition. I felt the Lord prompt me to pray trauma out of the arm, and the memory of the trauma out of the cells. Then she tried the arm again and could lift it up completely.

Lady from another faith healed

A lady came to the healing rooms and I was at the door as she left. She began to ask me questions about the heat that she was feeling in her shoulder, so I asked her what did she come to have prayer about. She shared with me that she had pain in her shoulder, so I was able to explain to her that it was the presence of the Lord touching the part of the body that needed healing. After sharing with her about the wonderful love of the Lord she left with tears streaming down her face.

Woman at meeting with rheumatoid arthritis

I was invited to be the speaker at a meeting in south London. In the ministry time afterwards a lady came forward with this arthritis in her knees. After praying there did not seem to be any improvement and as she walked away I could sense her disappointment. About six months later I was back in this same area and I met the same lady. As she approached me she began to share with me that the previous time I had prayed for her she did not have any apparent relief from the pain or any change in the mobility. Some weeks later she was out and she just knew she was healed and she was trying her leg for pain and there was none. It was gone. The Lord does not always answer our prayer for healing in the same way. He seems to have a variety of ways of ministering to us.

Legs growing out. The following is a testimony after prayer for this young man

"We saw God move in healing emotions and setting many free. One young person's leg grew 4 inches once he was prayed for. Previously, he had to walk on tip-toe due to the difference in the length of his legs and was due an operation.

After the healing, the hospital appointment and operations planned were cancelled and he also used that opportunity to witness to his friend".

Ears in Germany
We went to Norden, Germany with a friend from South Africa. In one of the meetings a lady was prayed for by Tom and me. She had problems with her ears and after prayer the problems left. She could now hear well and the discomfort was gone. As far as I know she is still healed today.

Ears healed
A lady testified that her six year old son was prayed for by two intercessors at the prayer room for his ears "to work properly". They rebuked the deaf and dumb spirit and prayed for healing.

As we walked outside the healing rooms my son immediately said that he could hear us talking even with the background noise (traffic).

Now he can hear speech clearly at a normal volume and he speaks much quieter.

The reason we can pray for healing.
The qualification we need and the authority we have.

MARK 16 v 15 -18
> [15] *And He said to them, "Go into all the world and preach the gospel to every creature.* [16] *He who believes and is baptized will be saved; but he who does not believe will be condemned.* [17] *And these signs will follow those who believe: In My name they will cast out demons; they will speak with new tongues;* [18] *they[b] will*

take up serpents; and if they drink anything deadly, it will
by no means hurt them; they will lay hands on the sick,
and they will recover."

The only qualification for ministering healing is as shown in
this passage, "He or she who believes". To believe means to
rely on, cling to or trust in, so anybody who has a trusting or
clinging relationship with the Lord can pray for the sick and
expect them to recover.

LUKE 10 v 18 – 19

[18] And He said to them, "I saw Satan fall like lightning
from heaven. [19] Behold, I give you the authority to trample
on serpents and scorpions, and over all the power of the
enemy, and nothing shall by any means hurt you.

The atonement

ISAIAH 53 (AMPLIFIED BIBLE)

[1]WHO HAS believed (trusted in, relied upon, and
clung to) our message [of that which was revealed
to us]? And to whom has the arm of the Lord been
disclosed? [2]For [the Servant of God] grew up before
Him like a tender plant, and like a root out of dry
ground; He has no form or comeliness [royal, kingly
pomp], that we should look at Him, and no beauty that
we should desire Him. [3]He was despised and rejected
and forsaken by men, a Man of sorrows and pains,
and acquainted with grief and sickness; and like One
from Whom men hide their faces He was despised, and
we did not appreciate His worth or have any esteem
for Him. [4]Surely He has borne our griefs (sicknesses,
weaknesses, and distresses) and carried our sorrows
and pains [of punishment], yet we [ignorantly]

considered Him stricken, smitten, and afflicted by
God [as if with leprosy]. *But He was wounded for
our transgressions, He was bruised for our guilt and
iniquities; the chastisement [needful to obtain] peace
and well-being for us was upon Him, and with the
stripes [that wounded] Him we are healed and made
whole. *All we like sheep have gone astray, we have
turned every one to his own way; and the Lord has
made to light upon Him the guilt and iniquity of us all.
*He was oppressed, [yet when] He was afflicted, He
was submissive and opened not His mouth; like a lamb
that is led to the slaughter, and as a sheep before her
shearers is dumb, so He opened not His mouth.

*By oppression and judgment He was taken
away; and as for His generation, who among them
considered that He was cut off out of the land of the
living [stricken to His death] for the transgression of
my [Isaiah's] people, to whom the stroke was due?
*And they assigned Him a grave with the wicked, and
with a rich man in His death, although He had done
no violence, neither was any deceit in His mouth. *Yet
it was the will of the Lord to bruise Him; He has put
Him to grief and made Him sick. When You and He
make His life an offering for sin [and He has risen
from the dead, in time to come], He shall see His
[spiritual] offspring, He shall prolong His days, and
the will and pleasure of the Lord shall prosper in His
hand. *He shall see [the fruit] of the travail of His
soul and be satisfied; by His knowledge of Himself
[which He possesses and imparts to others] shall My
[uncompromisingly] righteous One, My Servant, justify
many and make many righteous (upright and in right
standing with God), for He shall bear their iniquities
and their guilt [with the consequences, says the Lord].

The reason I have quoted this passage from the Amplified Bible is that this version of the Bible gives us all the possibilities of the Hebrew meanings. The Old Testament was written in Hebrew and as we look at the meanings of the words in detail we can see all the different human sufferings Jesus hung on the cross to make an atonement for. From these verses we can see that Jesus took our griefs, sorrows, pain, rejection, weaknesses, distresses, transgressions, iniquities and sins.

Some people may say, "well we cannot assume that these verses mean that, but we can see from the New Testament that Jesus interpreted this scripture himself."

MATTHEW 8 V 16 – 17

16 When evening had come, they brought to Him many who were demon-possessed. And He cast out the spirits with a word, and healed all who were sick, 17 that it might be fulfilled which was spoken by Isaiah the prophet, saying:
" He Himself took our infirmities
And bore our sicknesses."

So this leaves us in no doubt about what Isaiah 53 means. When praying for anybody, whether it is sickness or whatever, we need to have a scriptural basis for the ministry we do.

Really good news, the only qualification we need is to believe.

MARK V 16-20 (AMPLIFIED BIBLE)

16He who believes [who adheres to and trusts in and relies on the Gospel and Him Whom it sets forth] and is baptized will be saved [[l]from the penalty of eternal death]; but he who does not believe [who does not

adhere to and trust in and rely on the Gospel and Him
Whom it sets forth] will be condemned. [17]And these
attesting signs will accompany those who believe: in
My name they will drive out demons; they will speak
in new languages; [18]They will pick up serpents; and
[even] if they drink anything deadly, it will not hurt
them; they will lay their hands on the sick, and they
will get well. [19]So then the Lord Jesus, after He had
spoken to them, was taken up into heaven and He sat
down at the right hand of God.[C] [20]And they went out
and preached everywhere, while the Lord kept working
with them and confirming the message by the attesting
signs and miracles that closely accompanied [it].
Amen (so be it).

Isaiah 61 v 1

[1]THE SPIRIT of the Lord God is upon me, because the
Lord has anointed and qualified me to preach the Gospel
of good tidings to the meek, the poor, and afflicted; He
has sent me to bind up and heal the brokenhearted, to
proclaim liberty to the [physical and spiritual] captives
and the opening of the prison and of the eyes to those
who are bound,[A]

In Luke chapter 4 v 16 – 18, we see that Jesus Himself
quoted this passage and told everybody that He had now
fulfilled that scripture. The first thing He did when He came
down from the mount of temptation was to tell us what His
ministry to us is. He wants to heal all our broken pieces. I
remember when we first started the healing rooms I had a
vision of a large white plate, the kind you use for the turkey
at Christmas. This plate was picked up and thrown against
a wall and broke into a thousand pieces. That is what some
people's hearts are like, so broken by so many of the hurts,

disappointments and traumas of life, and of course if we
attend a church we often don't want to let anybody know
how we are really feeling, so we can put this mask on and
when anybody asks us how we are, we lie and say, "I'm fine".
We can be afraid of uncovering ourselves for fear of being
betrayed again. Any of us who does any kind of ministry
needs to be able to assure the person we are praying for that
we will never break their confidence or reveal to anybody
what they have shared. That can be fine until somebody well
known comes across our path. The temptation to share that
we have prayed for "so and so" is very strong, because it
will make us look so good. Many people have such traumas
that they have gone in very deep and a person may not
even remember the incident. We had a person come into the
rooms and one of the team heard the Holy Spirit say, "what
happened when you were 27?" The client could not remember
anything, so they went on praying about other things, but the
prompting about the age of 27 would not go away, so the
team member asked again, "what happened when you were
27?" Still no response. Just before the client left he said, "I
remember now", and they relayed a deep tragedy that had
happened. The team were able to minister to him by coming
against all the effects of this trauma, speaking healing to his
spirit and soul, and the client left having laid down a huge
burden at the foot of the cross.

I remember being in a healing room and a client came in
because of a damaged knee. While praying over the sheet the
client had filled in, one of the team heard the Holy Spirit say,
"tell them I said they will make it, they are not a failure, they
are not a useless or rubbish person". It turned out that earlier
in the afternoon this client's boss had said these exact words
to the client and had really cut into the client's heart and it
left them feeling very upset from this conversation. There
was no mention of this on the sheet they filled in, only the

physical complaint was there, but again the Holy Spirit sees and knows and cares about everything that has happened to us. I had such an impression of the Lord's compassion and His desire to heal and set us free from all that comes against us and hurts us. He wants us whole. This client had such an encounter with the Lord as we shared what He had said to us. They left the rooms walking on air, set free.

I remember on another occasion hearing and giving a word to a lady, "you are not ugly". The reaction of the lady concerned was that she was so touched by the Lord, she ended up slain in the Spirit, unable to stand but she had to just lie on the floor and soak up His wonderful presence. I must say I have only given this word the one time. And it was not particularly an easy word to give someone, but He knows best and when we are obedient to Him it is always such a blessing to everybody involved.

It seems sometimes to be the case, of course not always, that trauma can get very deep inside us, and cause our heart to break and even divide. This condition is called D.I.D. (dissociative identity disorder). A piece that is broken away can become distanced from the person, therefore they genuinely do not remember the incident. The Father has made within each one of us a way of escape so that when extremely painful incidents happen to us, for instance in war people have been tortured and the trauma can be so great, it becomes like it is happening to another person. Abuse in childhood, especially sexual over a long period of time, can cause a person to have a break within themselves. A lady in her fifties was prayed for and she had been through various therapies with not much freedom from the pain she carried. A word was given to ask her how was her relationship with her father. She was speechless for a moment and then she said, "how could you possibly know about my father?" This lovely lady had never told a single soul what happened between her and her father, about the long years and years of abuse from a toddler to a teenager, until she left home in fact. She had buried this information and the terrible emotions so deep in order to survive, a mechanism to keep one sane. The Lord began His work. The pieces could be brought back and healing could begin to take place. At the healing rooms we would not actually work through this process with a client as this is a professional and specially trained procedure. But we could recommend a person to continue their healing process with a specialist in this field and they could continue to come for support and prayer ministry while this is going on. We have seen this work very well. Often when in therapy sessions issues come up that cannot be dealt with by prayer in counselling sessions. We at the healing rooms can help a client bring these issues to Jesus and His wonderful healing balm can bring final restoration.

Not having a critical or judgemental attitude

MATTHEW 7 v 1 -5 (AMPLIFIED BIBLE)
1Do not judge and criticize and condemn others, so that you may not be judged and criticized and condemned yourselves. 2For just as you judge and criticize and condemn others, you will be judged and criticized and condemned, and in accordance with the measure you [use to] deal out to others, it will be dealt out again to you. 3Why do you [a]stare from without at the [b]very small particle that is in your brother's eye but do not become aware of and consider the beam [c]of timber that is in your own eye? 4Or how can you say to your brother, Let me get the tiny particle out of your eye, when there is the beam [d]of timber in your own eye? 5You hypocrite, first get the beam of timber out of your own eye, and then

you will see clearly to take the tiny particle out of your brother's eye.

Unity and transparency were the first words we heard when we were getting ready to open our healing rooms. The next thing the Lord said to us was the previous scripture was not to be judgemental.

Holloway prison

One of the things the Lord had led me into before I started the healing rooms was to be part of a chaplaincy team at Holloway prison on a voluntary basis. I loved this work so much, it was very rewarding. One of the most important lessons I learnt there was that I had a very judgemental attitude. I had judged so harshly people who had committed crimes. I just thought, lock them up and throw away the key. As I began to visit the girls in their cells, I listened to story upon story of awful circumstances that were experienced by the girls and so much lack of nurture, survivors taking all sorts of chemicals or alcohol, or maybe both to ease the pain they carried temporarily, fighting back at a horrible world of betrayal, being lied to, being walked out on, beaten or abused physically or verbally, facing temptations unprepared, seeing incidents no child should see, being abused in various ways for so long that eventually they become the abusers. Now I am not justifying crime of any kind at all, but we do have to take into account the bad starts people may have and the amount of overcoming they have to face is often difficult to imagine if you personally have been raised in a different fashion.

The Lord showed me a scenario like this......imagine two young girls. The one on the left was raised in a good Christian home, with two parents that were not dysfunctional, the relationships were open and safe, there was no abuse and they were not subject to evil influences. The one on the right had the exact opposite, she was raised by a prostitute on the streets, alcohol was available freely, smoking dope was a regular occurrence and many uncles around and all that goes with that. When the time comes for them both to walk with Jesus, the overcoming and scars to be healed of the girl on the right will be more challenging and difficult than the one on the left. Added onto all that, of course, the generational agreements in the family line will also be such a disadvantage. And from our safe and secure up-bringing we can judge the one on the right and expect them to act the same as us is a wrong judgement. Jesus never treated people the same, because He knew where they were coming from. He only asked one man to sell all he had and give to the poor. He did not ask that of everyone. He picked out the woman who gave a widow's mite and said, "she gave all she had". One person recited prayers of how glad they were that they were not like all the others around them and left the place of prayer with their prayers unanswered, but the one who knew they had sinned and cried out for mercy went home justified and free. The one who sinned most, loved most. One of the funny scenarios at the prison was learning not to laugh in the wrong place, which I'm still not sure I've mastered yet, because I am quite a graphic person, meaning I can picture the things you are telling me. I remember sitting on a cell bed with a lovely girl doing her time. She began to relate to me how her father was a roofer, who liked to have a drink or three, and one day he was doing a roofing job, and he had prepared a large container of very hot bitumen. Sadly, because of his drinking, he fell off the roof into the container of hot tar and he was spread-eagled for months in bandages. My sense of humour kicked in as I pictured this poor man all bandaged up from head to toe with just his eyes and mouth uncovered. It was hard not to see the funny side and not allow the smile to show, learning to grow in compassion, etc.

Prayer cloths

One of the surprising things for me was the way the Lord would use prayer cloths to touch and heal people.

ACTS 19 v 11-12 (NEW LIVING TRANSLATION)
> *[11] God gave Paul the power to perform unusual miracles.[12] When handkerchiefs or aprons that had merely touched his skin were placed on sick people, they were healed of their diseases, and evil spirits were expelled.*

When people have not been able to come to the Healing Rooms we will pray as a team over a piece of designated cloth in agreement and then it will be posted out or given to somebody to give to the person who needs a touch from the Lord. We have had amazing testimonies back from this procedure. We were invited to send a prayer cloth to Australia, to a man who had asbestosis. Apparently there is no cure for this disease of the lungs. After this man received the cloth and he placed it in a pyjama pocket, the next time he was tested there was no asbestosis. We have had many similar stories take place where the Lord has intervened into the situations of people's lives. A child came out of a six day coma after a cloth being put under the pillow or pinned to the bed sheet. A man came off a machine keeping him alive, when he was given 48 hours, otherwise they would turn off the machine. Perhaps one of the things the Lord likes is that when we send out a prayer cloth any of the team may have prayed over it, from the usual number of three team members to perhaps more in the worship time. Then nobody gets any glory for the healing or touch from the Lord because nobody knows which prayer, or which person, did the praying that brought the healing result. There are no stars in the Healing Rooms. The more humility we can walk in the better.

The prayer of agreement

Praying in threes
The reason why praying in threes is so good is because we can agree together as touching somebody, so fulfilling this scripture. It also means that we can have a man and two women, or two men and a woman, being careful not to have a man and a woman praying together on their own, unless they are a married couple, which would be very unwise, in the sense that it could lead to temptation. We have an enemy who would take advantage of any open doors he can find.

MATTHEW 18 v 18-20

[18] *"Assuredly, I say to you, whatever you bind on earth will be bound in heaven, and whatever you loose on earth will be loosed in heaven.*

[19] *"Again I say[a] to you that if two of you agree on earth as touching anything that they ask, it will be done for them by My Father in heaven.* [20] *For where two or three are gathered together in My name, I am there in the midst of them.*

Our agreement is in the name of Jesus Christ of Nazareth and His Word, not in the many denominations that we all come from, not in forms or rituals or the way we did it yesterday but only in the name that is above every name.

13 Learning to Flow With the Holy Spirit and His Gifts

ACTS 13:2-3 (NEW KING JAMES VERSION)
> *² As they ministered to the Lord and fasted, the Holy Spirit said, "Now separate to Me Barnabas and Saul for the work to which I have called them." ³ Then, having fasted and prayed, and laid hands on them, they sent them away.*

The Holy Spirit spoke and gave directions about who was to be sent. He was very specific. We should keep in mind what Jesus said, "I will build My Church". We are under His instruction, not our good ideas.

JOHN 10:27 (NEW KING JAMES VERSION)
> *²⁷ My sheep hear My voice, and I know them, and they follow Me.*

Hearing the voice of the Lord for ourselves is our inheritance. If it was true for Moses, Ezekiel and the disciples in the book of Acts, then it's also got to be true for us. Hearing can include seeing also, as some may hear by seeing what He is doing. Many of the gifts of the Spirit are hearing gifts. I Corinthians 12 lists nine gifts.

1.   *The word of wisdom*

In a situation we know just what to do, or we know what we should say, or in fact the way we should say it. Do we see or hear that wonderful gift or both? Sometimes it's just a knowing in our knower, i.e. deep on the inside. One cannot explain it easily, one just knows something is true.

2   *The word of knowledge*

The word of knowledge can be heard, seen or felt. In learning to operate in any gift, we can learn by getting it wrong, or by being afraid to act on what we get. I remember being at church and in the meeting the pastor asked if anybody had any words or felt the Holy Spirit was saying anything particular. I had this distinct feeling in one of my ears, but was too scared to say anything. It was before I got rid of the spirit of fear. At the end of the meeting I was standing near the door and a lady was saying to the pastor, "I have a terrible infection in my ear where I put in an earring and it has gone septic. Would you pray for my ear please?". Immediately I knew I had disobeyed the Lord by not bringing that word, because He obviously wanted to minister to that particular lady. So a lesson well learnt.

I remember walking down the road and seeing a name written over a person. I later found out that the name was correct. I could not have known this by any knowledge of my own.

Tom and I were buying the house we now live in. We went to the same Building Society that arranged the mortgage for the bookshop. They offered us a particular percentage of 5.9%. I was on a coach a few days later and I saw an advertisement in the newspaper by the same Building Society offering 5.79%. We went in immediately and explained what we saw. They agreed to that percentage. As Tom and I were listening to the financial advisor explaining everything to us, he began to say that we could have this rate of interest, which was a good rate for the time, for 3 years, 5 years or 7 years. I immediately thought, now this is such a good rate we should have it for the whole seven years. As I was explaining this to Tom and he agreed, I immediately felt on the inside, only take it for thee years. I foolishly thought to myself this cannot be right, as you would never get a better rate than this. Does the Holy Spirit know about money or not? So I disobeyed, never said anything to Tom, and we went ahead and signed for the seven years. Well I heard right, because after three years the interest rates fell drastically and we could have got another mortgage for a much lower rate of interest, but because of my thinking I knew better than God, Tom and I lost a lot of money because we had to carry on for the next 4 years paying the higher rate of interest. A costly learning curve, but a learning curve nonetheless. It also gave me confidence that I can hear the Lord accurately and that He does care and know about the everyday things of life.

Healing by the word of knowledge

I remember being in a restaurant. As I sat down with about 7 people I felt a particular feeling in my ankle. It was not a pain exactly, but a sense in the right ankle with a pain like feeling. I knew it would not stay, that once I had acted on it the feeling would leave. So I asked if anybody had something wrong with their right ankle. The person beside me piped up, yes I do. So we all prayed. Then I had the same kind of feeling in my left knee. I posed the same question and a person opposite responded to the question and we prayed for her. Often, if we would pay attention, we would realize the Lord is speaking to us. We often think, "it must be just me"!

3.   Faith
There is a gift of faith, like a higher level of faith that we can operate in, when you know beyond a shadow of a doubt that when you lay hands on somebody they are already healed, or a certain thing is going to happen.

4.   Gifts of healings operate in some people more than others
There have been many over the years like Kathryn Kuhlman, John Wimber, John. G. Lake, Smith Wigglesworth, Trevor Dearing, F.F. Bosworth, William Branham, Kenneth Hagin, Oral Roberts, to mention but a few. We can learn much from their writings and documented healings and miracles.

5.   To another the working of miracles
My understanding is that healings may take time, but miracles are instant. The story that I shared earlier about the boy with a leg 4 inches shorter than the other leg that lengthened instantly, I believe was a miracle. The ears that were restored in the ten year old girl was the working of a miracle. There are many more to come for us all if we press in.

6.   Prophecy
The Bible says we can all prophesy, but some stand in the office of a prophet. I believe that means that the prophecies a prophet will bring are very specific, and there is no doubt whether they are accurate or not because they will be proved whether they are accurate or not, because you will see if they come true or not.

    See an example in the following piece of Scripture.

1 SAMUEL 10 v 2-10

² When you have departed from me today, you will find two men by Rachel's Tomb in the territory of Benjamin at Zelzah; and they will say to you, 'The donkeys which you went to look for have been found. And now your father has ceased caring about the donkeys and is worrying about you, saying, "What shall I do about my son?"' ³ Then you shall go on forward from there and come to the terebinth tree of Tabor. There three men going up to God at Bethel will meet you, one carrying three young goats, another carrying three loaves of bread, and another carrying a skin of wine. ⁴ And they will greet you and give you two loaves of bread, which you shall receive from their hands. ⁵ After that you shall come to the hill of God where the Philistine garrison is. And it will happen, when you have come there to the city, that you will meet a group of prophets coming down from the high place with a stringed instrument, a tambourine, a flute, and a harp before them; and they will be prophesying. ⁶ Then the Spirit of the Lord will come upon you, and you will prophesy with them and be turned into another man. ⁷ And let it be, when these signs come to you, that you do as the occasion demands; for God is with you. ⁸ You shall go down before me to Gilgal; and surely I will come down to you to offer burnt offerings and make sacrifices of peace offerings. Seven days you shall wait, till I come to you and show you what you should do."

⁹ So it was, when he had turned his back to go from Samuel, that God gave him another heart; and all those signs came to pass that day. ¹⁰ When they came there to the hill, there was a group of prophets to meet him; then the Spirit of God came upon him, and he prophesied among them.

Of course is does happen that prophets can make mistakes too or mis-interpret what is being said, like this example:

Nathan the prophet, told David to do all that was in his heart when he wanted to build a temple for the Lord, then the Lord told him to tell him he could not build the temple, but Solomon his son would build it instead. But Nathan was still called a prophet even though he had to go back and correct his prophecy. Some people teach you can never make a mistake in your prophetic words but the Bible says otherwise:

2 SAMUEL 7 v 1 – 13

1 When King David was settled in his palace and the Lord had given him rest from all the surrounding enemies, 2 the king summoned Nathan the prophet. "Look," David said, "I am living in a beautiful cedar palace,[a] but the Ark of God is out there in a tent!" 3 Nathan replied to the king, "Go ahead and do whatever you have in mind, for the Lord is with you." 4 But that same night the Lord said to Nathan, 5 "Go and tell my servant David, 'This is what the Lord has declared: Are you the one to build a house for me to live in? 6 I have never lived in a house, from the day I brought the Israelites out of Egypt until this very day. I have always moved from one place to another with a tent and a Tabernacle as my dwelling. 7 Yet no matter where I have gone with the Israelites, I have never once complained to Israel's tribal leaders, the shepherds of my people Israel. I have never asked them, "Why haven't you built me a beautiful cedar house?"'

8 "Now go and say to my servant David, 'This is what the Lord of Heaven's Armies has declared: I took you from tending sheep in the pasture and selected you to be the leader of my people Israel. 9 I have been with you wherever you have gone, and I have destroyed all your

enemies before your eyes. Now I will make your name
as famous as anyone who has ever lived on the earth!
[10] And I will provide a homeland for my people Israel,
planting them in a secure place where they will never
be disturbed. Evil nations won't oppress them as they've
done in the past, [11] starting from the time I appointed
judges to rule my people Israel. And I will give you rest
from all your enemies.
  "'Furthermore, the Lord declares that he will make
a house for you—a dynasty of kings! [12] For when you
die and are buried with your ancestors, I will raise up
one of your descendants, your own offspring, and I will
make his kingdom strong. [13] He is the one who will build
a house—a temple—for my name. And I will secure his
royal throne forever."

ACTS 2 V 17

And it shall come to pass in the last days, says God, That
I will pour out of My Spirit on all flesh; Your sons and
your daughters shall prophesy, Your young men shall see
visions, Your old men shall dream dreams

1 CORINTHIANS 14:31

[31]For ye may all prophesy one by one, that all may learn,
and all may be comforted.

I have had some very accurate prophecies from people who
would not call themselves a prophet.

7. *Discerning of spirits*

Discernment is a very necessary gift to operate in. We can
save ourselves lots of time, energy and wasted journeys if
we would learn to discern and take notice of what we are
discerning. Many times we discern but do not recognize it.

How many times have we said, "I had this feeling in the pit of my stomach and chose to ignore it" and the thing went wrong.

HEBREWS 5 v 13-14 (AMPLIFIED BIBLE)
13For everyone who continues to feed on milk is obviously inexperienced and unskilled in the doctrine of righteousness (of conformity to the divine will in purpose, thought, and action), for he is a mere infant [not able to talk yet]! 14But solid food is for full-grown men, for those whose senses and mental faculties are trained by practice to discriminate and distinguish between what is morally good and noble and what is evil and contrary either to divine or human law.

This verse tells us discernment is about practising and training our physical senses, very much like what I was saying about feeling in our own bodies pain or noticing a particular part of our body. These gifts do run one into the other and often are hard to distinguish and divide.

We can learn to discern angels, demons, know when people are oppressed, we can know if somebody is telling the truth or not. This can be seeing or feeling, or sensing. But practice is important because we get to know how the Lord will work with us by practice. There are times when I can feel different things in different hands and I know by those feelings what that means. But this is learnt over a period of time by working and asking questions of the Holy Spirit. He will tell us what each thing means. We can discern His presence in a place. Or likewise the evil one in a place, person or thing. We can see darkness or blackness around a particular thing or place. This is a gift we need to utilize in these days so we don't get deceived or led up the garden path.

8. Tongues
When we don't know how to pray for a situation, we can use the gift of tongues to intercede.

ROMANS 8 V 26 (AMPLIFIED BIBLE)
²⁶So too the [Holy] Spirit comes to our aid and bears us up in our weakness; for we do not know what prayer to offer nor how to offer it worthily as we ought, but the Spirit Himself goes to meet our supplication and pleads in our behalf with unspeakable yearnings and groanings too deep for utterance.

Using the gift of tongues in our private devotions can lift us into a deeper place in the Spirit and can be the doorway to the other gifts.

In 1 Corinthians 14 v 18 the Apostle Paul said, "I thank my God, I speak with tongues more than you all." I have already written about the time the man came in with the gun, and how I prayed in tongues loudly and frightened him away.

When Tom was at work on a night shift, there were times of being alone by myself with the children. When I would feel afraid I would go downstairs and read Psalm 91 out loud and pray in tongues. Shortly after, the fear of being alone would leave.

9. Interpretation of tongues
In worship times with other Christians one can feel gently pressed to speak in a tongue out loud by yourself. Somebody in the room may get words that are the interpretation of those tongues. Often the gifts of the Holy Spirit come in the form of one word and then as you take a step of faith the other words follow. It can be like that with the gift of tongues too. I remember complaining to the Lord that I only had a few words when

I was comparing myself with others I could hear, but He instantly gently told me off with, "you are not using what you have already", and as I use that gift frequently it has developed into several languages.

Jig saw puzzle

Each thing the Lord teaches us and the things we experience are like a giant jigsaw puzzle and we learn piece by piece. We cannot put certain pieces into place until others are in place first. For instance, I could not have run healing rooms without having been part of certain churches where I learnt so much for my journey. I am grateful for every pastor and leader I have had over the thirty five years since Jesus began to take hold of me. I could not have missed out on one as I was fed and nurtured and taught so much. If any of you leaders are reading this book, can I say thank you so much for your input into my life.

The role of the leader

EPHESIANS 4 V 7-16 – SPIRITUAL GIFTS

> [7] *But to each one of us grace was given according to the measure of Christ's gift.* [8] *Therefore He says:*
> *When He ascended on high,*
> *He led captivity captive,*
> *And gave gifts to men."*[b]
> [9] *(Now this, "He ascended"—what does it mean but that He also first*[c] *descended into the lower parts of the earth?* [10] *He who descended is also the One who ascended far above all the heavens, that He might fill all things.)*
> [11] *And He Himself gave some to be apostles, some prophets, some evangelists, and some pastors and*

teachers, [12] for the equipping of the saints for the work
of ministry, for the edifying of the body of Christ, [13] till
we all come to the unity of the faith and of the knowledge
of the Son of God, to a perfect man, to the measure of
the stature of the fullness of Christ; [14] that we should no
longer be children, tossed to and fro and carried about
with every wind of doctrine, by the trickery of men, in the
cunning craftiness of deceitful plotting, [15] but, speaking
the truth in love, may grow up in all things into Him
who is the head—Christ— [16] from whom the whole body,
joined and knit together by what every joint supplies,
according to the effective working by which every part
does its share, causes growth of the body for the edifying
of itself in love.

I was raised by wonderful Christian teachers and had such a lot of very good teaching that was invaluable. I have observed over the years that some of the life of the Church may be restricting because the leaders can do most of the ministry or have a tendency to be controlling. We were taught that we were there to serve the leaders. And that will always be true, but the opposite is true also.

EPHESIANS 4 v 11 – 12
[11] And He Himself gave some to be apostles, some
prophets, some evangelists, and some pastors and
teachers, [12] for the equipping of the saints for the work of
ministry, for the edifying of the body of Christ,

According to these verses, the hand of the Lord, the five fingers, represent the functions of the five fold ministry, each finger and thumb representing one of these five offices. They are there to equip, to recognize and bring out the gifts that are already within the person and to teach them how to function in those gifts and bring them to a place of maturity. Therefore the five fold ministers are there to serve the body rather than to be served. Just like Jesus, He said he came to serve rather than to be served. He demonstrated that when He took a towel.

JOHN 13 V 3-17 (NEW KING JAMES VERSION)

³ Jesus, knowing that the Father had given all things into His hands, and that He had come from God and was going to God, ⁴ rose from supper and laid aside His garments, took a towel and girded Himself. ⁵ After that, He poured water into a basin and began to wash the disciples' feet, and to wipe them with the towel with which He was girded. ⁶ Then He came to Simon Peter. And Peter said to Him, "Lord, are You washing my feet?"

⁷ Jesus answered and said to him, "What I am doing you do not understand now, but you will know after this." ⁸ Peter said to Him, "You shall never wash my feet!" Jesus answered him, "If I do not wash you, you have no part with Me."

⁹ Simon Peter said to Him, "Lord, not my feet only, but also my hands and my head!"

¹⁰ Jesus said to him, "He who is bathed needs only to wash his feet, but is completely clean; and you are clean, but not all of you." ¹¹ For He knew who would betray Him; therefore He said, "You are not all clean."

¹² So when He had washed their feet, taken His garments, and sat down again, He said to them, "Do you know what I have done to you? ¹³ You call Me Teacher and Lord, and you say well, for so I am. ¹⁴ If I then, your Lord and Teacher, have washed your feet, you also ought to wash one another's feet. ¹⁵ For I have given you an example, that you should do as I have done to you. ¹⁶

Most assuredly, I say to you, a servant is not greater than his master; nor is he who is sent greater than he who sent him. [17] *If you know these things, blessed are you if you do them.*

One of the most thrilling things for me as a leader in the Healing Rooms is when we recognize people coming in to join our team, and as they come week by week we see the transformation and growth that takes place from being in a greenhouse. The gifts begin to flourish and they become so confident in their ability to hear the Lord and to step out and see how the Lord can use them.

No feelings for three years

Normally I am a touchy, feely person. What I mean is, normally I can feel the presence of the Lord around. I have always been very sensitive to His touch. The Lord seemed to tell me that I would not have that any more for a season. This season lasted for about three years. It was very strange at first, but then I got used to just believing He was with me, because He said in His Word that He would never leave me nor forsake me (Hebrews 13 v 5). So I had to learn to just take Him at His Word and not depend on my feelings. This was a very good but hard lesson to learn, because we have to learn to walk by faith and not by sight or feelings. My trust in His Word grew and grew. This is one of the reasons I quote so much scripture in my book. I believe nothing is in there by accident; it is there for our benefit. I never pray, "Lord please be with so and so". That is a prayer of unbelief, because He says He will never leave us "until the end of the world", Matthew 28 v 20. He likes to be believed.

Where the Church is at right now

About four years ago, I saw a running vision of the shape and outline of what we would consider to be a normal church building, very much like the shapes one sees in villages in England. As I watched the church building, it began to fall down and there was a lot of dust and bricks flying about everywhere. Everything was very dusty and messy, and then I saw the Lord come and pick up the bricks from amongst the dust and begin to make a different shape of building out of the bricks. The new building was completely different and quite un-recognizable from the older one. I sense also that the day of the one man band type ministry is coming slowly to an end, and is being replaced with an army of people, trained up ready to be able to step into any spiritual situation and obey the Lord's direction, to see His power flow through the ordinary believer, the one without any kind of qualifications other than they believe. I believe we are heading towards that day when these words of Jesus will be fulfilled again by anybody who truly believes.

JOHN 14:11-13 (NEW KING JAMES VERSION)
¹¹ Believe Me that I am in the Father and the Father in Me, or else believe Me for the sake of the works themselves. ¹² "Most assuredly, I say to you, he who believes in Me, the works that I do he will do also; and greater works than these he will do, because I go to My Father. ¹³ And whatever you ask in My name, that I will do, that the Father may be glorified in the Son.

One of the things we are learning is not to have an agenda about how to pray for a person. We cannot in our own strength see or know what a person may need, beyond what

LEARNING TO FLOW WITH THE HOLY SPIRIT AND HIS GIFTS   135

our physical eyes may see, as only the Lord knows what they really need right now.

Testing prophecies

Although I have given a lot of examples from my own life about the wonderful prophecies I have received and the accuracy they contained, and the wonderful help they have been to me, I must also put a caution in here for the sake of you who read my book. This gift can be very destructive and also can be counterfeited. The Bible tells us we must test all prophecy. This is where the gift of discerning of spirits comes in. We need to know what spirit is operating. We need to use a lot of wisdom in the giving and receiving of prophecies. I would recommend when we are around people we don't know, if somebody says they have a word for us, then to ask them to hold on a minute and get somebody you know to be there with you. That helps a lot in the accurate testing of the words given. The Bible says that the words of the prophet are subject to the prophet. Therefore, that means if the person giving the word is not healed up on the inside and still is walking in unforgiveness or bitterness, that can come across in the prophecies they give. If they have particular ideas or strong opinions, that can colour what they give. Remember, we are human beings with many faults and wrong belief systems. These faults can get into and frame all the words we speak including the colouring of the words we give. There are some good boundaries in this area that I have put in place in the healing rooms.

Dates........People can put a date on a word. i.e. "by next year you will have experienced" ....or "in seven days such and such will happen"............

There may be occasions when this is correct but I have found that putting a date on a word limits it. For example, our healing rooms were given a word that I believe is true but the person put on it that it had to happen this summer. That was three years ago and it has not happened yet. I believe it is a true word from God, but the time is not yet.

Births......It could be very dangerous to give or receive a prophetic word about having babies. Married couples who are believing to conceive a child are very vulnerable and we need to be extremely careful about giving words and receiving words in this situation. Having someone you know well with you would be very wise.

Marriages......This could be one of the abuses of the gift of prophecy. I have watched many people be devastated and even walk away from the Lord over this issue. I watched one young man receive a word from somebody that he was just about to meet his wife. He began looking and as a result of that looking became entangled unsuitably, believing the Lord wanted him to marry a particular lady. This would have been disastrous. So again, do not receive such a word from anybody, (even if they tell you they are Elijah the prophet). Stop them and explain that you want your pastor or leader present first. That usually will show whether this is true word or not and will save much pain. The most dangerous people to operate in the gifts of the Spirit are those people who have a need to be recognized, to be seen to be somebody special. This need will push people to give imaginary words because they are so needy for approval and the desire to be well thought of and accepted. I am not saying that the Lord would never speak to somebody concerning these three things but such words would need to come from a prophet who is recognized as such by the Body of Christ, who is accountable and correctable, with a mature leader or pastor present to give counsel and advice afterwards. It is so easy for us to rattle off words but the consequences can devastate a life permanently.

Praying in supermarkets and out and about

One of the most rewarding ways to reach people and see them touched for the Lord is to ask Him to give us words of knowledge while out shopping. I have found myself in queues and knowing the person in front is in pain, asking them, "are you in any pain by any chance?" When finding out you heard the Lord correctly, and offering to pray, oftentimes the person will say yes. And the surprise when you begin to pray on the spot. "What now?" and then I would ask, "Is there any pain there now?" You can see the look of surprise in their eyes, because they can't feel the pain and they stay trying to find it, by pushing the part of the body that had the pain. "No. It seems to have gone". One of my favourites was the following day after a dream in the night of ministering in a local shop and out in the open air. I saw a lady at a pier, and after a little conversation she said she would so love to have Jesus in her heart and life. After praying with her, she was so thrilled to know she did not have to fear death, as she had really carried a great fear of that. She hugged me as I left her to go on with the Lord. One day we will meet again, not at the pier but at the throne or some other place in the heavenly realms. Our treasures are there waiting for us. Perhaps I will be able to invite her to my house in heaven and we can smile, remembering that day especially arranged for her.

Accusations

One of the main schemes the enemy uses to attack us and try to stop us going on with the Lord is the accusations of our past failures. If our families, or children, are not happy about some mistakes they perceive we have made as parents or grandparents, this is one of the enemy's most painful attacks. It can cause us to carry guilt and to feel a failure. Every time we try to step out in obedience to the Lord for some new assignment up come the reminders of the past failures and mistakes, and we have to deal with it all over again, the unfairness we feel, the lack of recognition of the sacrifices we have made to bring up our children and to give them our perceived best. I realize that this is only because they are in pain, because of our mistakes, or perceived mistakes. This can be like a black cloud that hangs over us and can be very hard to overcome, and having overcome for a time, visits to children in their homes, or their visits to us, can bring it all back and we have to start again. In one of our worship times in the healing rooms, one of the team had the following impression from the Lord. Like David had stones to throw at Goliath, the Lord showed us to prophetically pick up stones and throw them at our own "Goliaths", whatever they may be. We can deal with the accuser in whatever way we feel led, as long as we do it, and not allow him to get away with it. I just have to keep remembering that all my past is forgiven and washed away. Resentment carried by anybody drives them to keep punishing us, keep snide and disrespectful remarks coming. No wonder the Bible tells us there is long life for those who honour their parents. The Lord is so kind, when we go through this, especially as mothers or fathers. The Lord can send somebody to us. I know of one parent who, when going through this, He sent two different people who did not have any idea what they were going through, or the enormous pain they felt. The Lord told them to say to the mother (in this case), "the Lord says you were a good mother", then the choice is whether to believe the Lord or the offspring.

Bookshop award, 2008

We were nominated for the large retailer of the year. Over the thirty years or so we have been running the Good News Shop, we have seen different bookshops being nominated for the "Christian bookseller of the year award" and finally came our turn. In 2008 we were nominated and to our delight we won. It was such a good feeling of recognition and appreciation of the last 30 years of hard work.

Receiving the award for best bookshop of the year, 2008

14 *My Final Words To You*

|||||||||||||||||||||||||||||||||||||||||||||||||||||||||||||||||||||||||||||||||||||||||||||||||||||||||

In 1977, having listened to Trevor Dearing (an Anglican minister much used by the Lord) talk about a hairdresser who shared Jesus with her customers, how many came to Him in her business, Trevor began to go on to talk about the feeding of the five thousand.

JOHN 6 V 5 V 14 (NEW KING JAMES VERSION)
*Then Jesus lifted up His eyes, and seeing a great
multitude coming toward Him, He said to Philip, "Where
shall we buy bread, that these may eat?" ⁶ But this He
said to test him, for He Himself knew what He would do.
⁷ Philip answered Him, "Two hundred denarii worth of
bread is not sufficient for them, that every one of them
may have a little."*

*⁸ One of His disciples, Andrew, Simon Peter's
brother, said to Him, ⁹ "There is a lad here who has
five barley loaves and two small fish, but what are they
among so many?"*

*¹⁰ Then Jesus said, "Make the people sit down."
Now there was much grass in the place. So the men sat
down, in number about five thousand. ¹¹ And Jesus took
the loaves, and when He had given thanks He distributed
them to the disciples, and the disciples[a] to those sitting
down; and likewise of the fish, as much as they wanted.*

141

*[12] So when they were filled, He said to His disciples,
"Gather up the fragments that remain, so that nothing
is lost." [13] Therefore they gathered them up, and filled
twelve baskets with the fragments of the five barley
loaves which were left over by those who had eaten. [14]
Then those men, when they had seen the sign that Jesus
did, said, "This is truly the Prophet who is to come into
the world."*

I was so touched as Trevor shared about how something so
small that we may have or own, or just ourselves, when we
put it all into the hands of Jesus, what He can do with it.
Remember the little boy's lunch was all he had. Probably
his mother made it that day for him. He was hungry. Think
how he trusted Jesus, how his little eyes must have watched
it disappear in the master's hands, all broken up and divided
into twelve hands to be given to this gigantic crowd. How
did this little boy feel? Did he think it is insane trying to
make this little lunch feed this many people? His eyes must
have got bigger and bigger as he watched it never stop being
there, how there was so much that even some fell onto the
ground as it does when there is plenty, how Jesus can make
our little offerings go further than our wildest imaginations.
I was so touched by this message, that all I could do was
kneel down on the floor by the settee I had been sitting on
listening to this message. I began to give Jesus our little
shop that sold cigarettes and told Him if there is anything
You can do with this 14ft x 12ft shop then please take it
and do with it what You will. A few short years later He
took us up on that, and then as I have already shared with
you, came the conviction to stop selling the ciggies, then
the bookshop was born, then the extension came, then the
healing rooms, with between 40 and 60 people being prayed
for every week, some even giving their lives to Jesus for

the first time. What I gave Jesus all those years ago, He has multiplied far beyond my wildest dreams and imaginations. As I end my story for now, I would encourage you firstly, if you have not made Jesus your Lord, to do just that, and then to put into His hands anything and everything you have and are, and just watch as He multiplies it far beyond anything you could ever imagine. If you keep it for yourself then it remains just yours. He is the same, yesterday, today and forever, and He can take fish and bread, such an everyday familiar thing, bless it, and break it to be shared out among others to fill them to the full. Jesus had such respect for the little boy's offering, that he had the disciples gather up every crumb, so that nothing of the offering was wasted. He treats what we give Him exactly the same way. He wastes nothing. He does not allow it to be trampled on. Oh, there may be the breaking of it, but that is only for distribution and to get rid of the pride, but He treasures what we lay at His feet. Just watch what He will do with the offering of your life, your property, all that you have, and the rich treasure you will have now and waiting for you in that place we call heaven. The Lord bless you as you give Him your loaves and fishes, and all that you are.

Have fun and enjoy your life.

Betty Burke

A ministry session at the Healing Rooms

We hope you enjoyed reading this
New Wine book.
For details of other New Wine books
and a wide range of titles from other
Word and Spirit publishers visit our website:
www.newwineministries.co.uk
or email us at newwine@xalt.co.uk